Praise for *The Miracle Boy*

"Irelan's humanity, acute sense of humor, and mastery of timing should give this collection broad appeal among readers of short fiction."

—*Booklist* (ALA)

"This plainspoken and quirky collection is imbued with a wit as comfortable as an evening with Garrison Keillor."

—*Foreword Reviews*

"You know when you were a kid and your dad drove too fast over the crest of a hill and it felt like the car was leaving the ground, you'd get a tickle in the back of your throat and a tingle between your legs? That's what Patrick Irelan's stories do to your mind. *Miracle Boy* is a great ride."

—J. Harley McIlrath, author, *Possum Trot*

"Irelan is a fascinating storyteller who sets his tales in small and tiny ideas but with large themes: A kid walks on water, and an entrepreneur makes his fortune selling adulterated Dr Pepper to tourists in Branson. These stories join the absurd with reality, which is remarkably close to Vonnegut territory. So it goes."

— ꓺkstore

"In Patrick Irelan's new short story collection, *The Miracle Boy*, it doesn't take long for the magical to seem ordinary, and pretty soon the ordinary becomes magical. It's a collection of humor and wonder that will make you take a fresh look at the world around you."

—Jim O'Loughlin, Professor in the Department of Languages & Literature, University of Northern Iowa

"What if we had the ability to make our dreams come true? In the tradition of Jonathan Swift, these stories challenge both our hopes and dreams."

—Richard Burgin, Editor, *Boulevard Magazine*

"Irreverent and imaginative, these are very funny stories. They satirize the current state of affairs in our beloved nation, and like all good satire they include a tone of lament: they weep for an America that (perhaps) once was, and for the America it might—with better luck—have become. Read 'em and laugh."

—Dan Lechay, author of *The Quarry*, Ohio University Press Poetry Series

THE MIRACLE BOY

STORIES BY
PATRICK IRELAN

ICE CUBE PRESS, LLC, EST. 1993
NORTH LIBERTY, IOWA

The Miracle Boy—Stories by Patrick Irelan

Copyright © 2013 Patrick Irelan

Isbn 9781888160765   1 3 5 7 9 8 6 4 2

Library of Congress Preassigned Number: 2013937027

Ice Cube Press, LLC (Est. 1993)
205 N. Front Street
North Liberty, Iowa 52317
w: www.icecubepress.com
e: steve@icecubepress.com
twitter: @icecubepress

The paper used in this publication meets the minimum requirements of the American National Standard for Information Sciences— Permanence of Paper for Printed Library Materials, ANSI Z39.48- 1992.

Manufactured in the United States of America with recycled paper.

Some of these stories first appeared in literary journals and maga- zines—"The Lily of the West" in *The Wapsipinicon Almanac*; "The Sheep" in Skive; "David's Toe" in *Crosscurrents*; and "The Witness" and "New Money" in *EQMM*. "The Miracle Boy" and "Palermo Coffee" ap- peared online at *Defenestration* and *Marguerite Avenue*, respectively.

TO
CLAIRE
AND
EMILY

Into my heart an air that kills
From yon far country blows:
What are those blue remembered hills,
What spires, what farms are those?

    —A.E. Housman

CONTENTS

THE MIRACLE BOY

When I was fourteen years old, I began walking on water. My parents watched me walk back and forth across the pond a few times. "Angie," Dad said, "this looks like a miracle."

"Sure does," Mom said. "Good job, Michael." Then they went back to the house and sat down to figure out the profit angle. Mom and Dad were always looking for ways to make money on the farm. The hills made the place picturesque, but the soil was worthless.

Dad went into Clearfield and got three hundred dollars in change while my mom called KTVO and all the neighbors. The neighbors came right over, watched me walk on the water, and said they'd tell everyone they knew. Then Dad mowed half the hayfield north of the pond lot.

While Dad was still in the hayfield, a guy with a KTVO television camera and a woman with a microphone got set up to interview me. I walked slowly on the water along the pond bank while the woman asked questions. Then the guy with the camera tripped on something and fell into the pond. The woman and the camera guy started yelling at each other, and the redwings in the cattails flew off into the cottonwood trees. Finally, the guy found another camera and we started over again.

"How long have you been doing this?" the woman said.

"Just since this morning," I said. I glanced at the woman when I answered her questions. She was kind of cute for an adult, with blue eyes and curly blond hair.

She wasn't as cute as Katie, though. No one was. Katie was my secret girlfriend. She had to be a secret because her parents said she was too young to have a boyfriend and go out on dates. I couldn't go out on dates anyway. Katie lived in town, and I lived on the farm. It was too far to walk, and I wasn't old enough to drive anything but our John Deere tractor. Katie said her parents wouldn't like it if I parked a tractor on the driveway.

So we just hung out together at Fox County High School, where we were both freshmen, and where most of the other kids soon discovered our secret. Katie had brown eyes, long black hair with a natural wave, and a nose like one you'd see on the statue of a Greek goddess. Her face was so beautiful that I thought about her all the time. Walking on water was kind of fun, but merely holding hands with Katie was my idea of what heaven should be like. And when she opened her locker, hid behind the door, and let me kiss her, I had feelings I still can't describe.

Anyway, I talked to the woman from KTVO, and that night Mom, Dad, my little sister, and I all watched the ten o'clock news. The cameraman hadn't fallen into the pond again, so we all got a good look at my walking skills. My sister, whose name is Thelma, got jealous because I was famous and she wasn't. I told her you had to be fourteen before you could walk on water, and that she could barely walk on dry land. Mom said, "Pipe down, you two. Your father and I have to sit down again and make plans."

Thelma went into her room and slammed the door, and I went outside and walked around the yard in the darkness, thinking about Katie. Off in the distance to the south, I could see the illuminated clock tower of the Fox County Courthouse in Clearfield. The bell would ring eleven times at eleven o'clock. It was time to do my homework for freshman algebra, but all I could think about was Katie.

The next day, Thelma had to catch the school bus, but the folks kept me home, even though I'd stayed up late to do my algebra assignment. "Today's Friday," Dad said. "It won't hurt you to miss another day."

After getting Thelma onto the school bus, Mom set up a card table on the lawn, right beside the gravel lane that connected our house to the county's blacktop road. Then she put a cashbox on the table and sat down on a lawn chair. Thanks to the KTVO news story, the cars started coming down the lane at about nine o'clock, and Mom collected the money while Dad directed traffic into the hayfield, which he now called the parking lot. Traffic on the county road at the other end of the lane got so heavy that two deputy sheriffs came out, waved their arms, and pointed first one direction then another.

Mom charged five dollars per car plus two dollars for adults and one dollar for children. Some people tried to park along the blacktop road so they wouldn't have to pay to park the car, but the deputies told them the road wasn't a parking lot and get moving.

I had a pretty good time. I walked awhile. Then I did some somersaults and cartwheels. I tried to walk on my hands, but I wasn't any good at it. One little kid said this was boring, but his mom slapped the side of his head and told him to shut up and pay attention.

One of the deputies came down the lane about four o'clock that afternoon and said they couldn't stay all night, so the folks stuck a "Closed" sign on the mailbox, and I walked away from the pond.

The next day, which was Saturday, we had everything better organized. Aunt Mary and Uncle Floyd came over with hotdogs, buns, potato chips, ice tea, and beer. One of the deputies said they'd better have a liquor license, which they didn't. So Uncle Floyd started drinking the beer himself, and by two o'clock Aunt Mary told him he was no help at all and get out of the way.

Uncle Floyd was my mom's brother. He was six-four, had a bulbous nose, and always wore his pants about five inches too short. When anyone asked why his pants were so short, he said, "To keep my ankles cool."

Aunt Mary was a foot shorter than Uncle Floyd and had a florid complexion that made everyone say she had great circulation and would live forever. After I started walking on water, Aunt Mary said one miracle in the family was enough and she didn't need to live forever.

My parents had been good-looking when their wedding pictures were taken, but they hadn't aged well. My dad had too much belly, and my mom had too many chins.

By the middle of the afternoon, I started to get tired of everything. The little kids kept telling me to do stupid things I couldn't do, and I finally said, "Why don't you little farts go drown yourselves."

I got a few laughs from that, but one of the mothers went and complained to Aunt Mary. This woke up Uncle Floyd, who told the woman to stop talking about his nephew and get her little brat away from the pond if he didn't like the show. Then the kid's dad came over and said, "Don't talk that way to my wife."

Uncle Floyd was big and strong, and could handle himself pretty well, even when he was drunk, which was most of the time. "I'll talk anyway I want," he said.

Then Dad came over and gave the man back his money and told him to go home and teach his kid some manners. So the man and woman left with their brat, and Uncle Floyd said, "Good work, Lester," and went back to sleep.

The next day, Uncle Floyd bribed someone in Des Moines and got a liquor license in record time, even though it was Sunday and the state offices were supposed to be closed. Mom said that it was a bigger miracle than walking on water. "Now all you have to do is stay sober and don't drink up all the profits," she said to Uncle Floyd. She was his older sister, and he always did what she said. He sold so much beer that the tavern owners in town complained about it, even though they weren't open on Sunday.

At five o'clock that afternoon, the sheriff drove down the lane and said the board of supervisors was griping about paying the deputies when all they did was direct traffic for our little field of dreams. He said he only had three deputies and the folks would have to hire some off-duty police from Ottumwa or call off the show. He gave them some phone numbers, and they got two young guys for Monday. Aunt Mary said she'd give them free hotdogs, but Uncle Floyd said they'd have to buy their own beer.

The folks kept me home again on Monday. I liked making money for them. We never had enough because the only thing that would grow on our hills was livestock, which in our case was hogs and beef cattle. I didn't care if I missed school, but I really wanted to see Katie more than I wanted the money.

By this time, there were so many people coming to see the show that the traffic was backed up all the way to Highway 63. The old people said there hadn't been that much traffic in Iowa since Roswell Garst brought Nikita Khrushchev over from Russia to buy Garst's hybrid seed corn.

About one o'clock that afternoon, Mom said she had so much money that she was afraid to take it to the bank by herself. So one of the policemen from Ottumwa drove her to the bank in Clearfield, and she gave him an apple pie to take home with him. Uncle Floyd gave him all the free beer he could drink, and about two hours later, the policeman went to sleep in the haymow.

Dad said, "Now look here, Floyd. Am I supposed to pay that man for sleeping all afternoon? And now we got only one guy to direct traffic the rest of the day."

"All right, all right, Lester," Uncle Floyd said. "Mary can sell the hotdogs and beer, and I'll direct traffic." This worked okay until Uncle Floyd got drunk on the twelve-pack he carried around with him. Then he started directing people into the hog lot instead of the hayfield, and they all got their cars stuck in the mud. Then the women complained about getting mud on their shoes, and Dad said he'd get the tractor and pull their cars out and we wouldn't charge them anything to see the show.

By Tuesday, Dad had mowed the rest of the hayfield, and the parking lot had grown to about twenty acres. We had eight off-duty policemen to direct traffic and keep order. The Burlington Northern Santa Fe Railroad was delivering carloads of hotdogs to Ottumwa, where Uncle Floyd picked them up with his cattle truck. He always got drunk while driving the twenty miles back to the farm, but Mom didn't know about it. She was too busy taking care of the money.

The weather turned hot, and the Fox County Hospital set up an infirmary in the barn to take care of the folks who got sick. People from all over were saying that I was destined for sainthood. Father Rossi said he would definitely talk to the bishop of the Davenport Diocese, but he reminded everyone that it usually took the Church a long time to beatify anyone, and besides that I was a Methodist.

"What if we all convert?" Dad said.

"That would be fine with me, Lester," Father Rossi said, "but it won't guarantee sainthood for anyone."

Mom said it might be good for business if we all converted, but we'd have to keep it a secret from the Methodists.

All the adults in the family thought they had come up with some real good ways to improve the business, but I was starting to get sick of the whole thing. I felt like a monkey, walking back and forth on the water all day, with people pointing at me and taking pictures. Then the high-school principal called one night to ask why I wasn't going to school. "We're converting to a new religion," Dad said, "and we're spending all our time in prayer and meditation."

My dad hadn't spent a minute of time in prayer and meditation in his whole life, and the principal, like everyone else in the state, knew exactly what was going on at our pond. The speaker phone was turned on, so all of us could hear Mrs. Fleming's voice. "Mister Hudgens," she said, "the laws of Iowa say that all children must attend school until they reach the age of sixteen. There are exceptions, of course, for children with medical problems or other relevant conditions, but converting to a new religion doesn't qualify for one of those exceptions. If Michael isn't back in school by Monday at the latest, I'll have no choice but to initiate the appropriate legal proceedings. Goodbye."

Dad's body slumped a little as he hung up the phone. "Lester," Aunt Mary said, "that business about prayer and meditation is the stupidest idea I've ever heard. An average chipmunk could've thought of something better."

"It's not easy explaining things to high-school principals," Dad said. "All they ever talk about is school and students."

Mom said that Dad did the best he could, and Aunt Mary said that wasn't much.

"We'll just have to do the show on weekends from now on," Dad said, but he was wrong again. The next morning, I started walking across the pond and quickly noticed that my shoes were filling up with water. I was walking in the pond, not on it. The miracle had ended.

"That does it," Mom said. "Floyd, go down to the other end of the lane and put the 'Closed' sign on the mailbox. Michael, go get ready for school."

⊚ ⊚ ⊚

I've never been as happy to go back to school as I was that day. The teachers pretended that nothing unusual had happened as they piled on all the homework I had to do.

The boys were all as bad as I knew they'd be. They called me "Saint Michael," "Your Sainthood," and other things they thought were so funny. But the girls were interested in a different subject. "Katie has a new boyfriend," one of them said. "She never wants to see you again." Every girl I saw started giggling as if I was a new life form from Comedy Central.

But when I finally caught sight of Katie, she broke all kinds of rules and ran the length of the hallway and would have knocked me down if I hadn't bent forward and braced myself. She kissed me as she never had before, and I didn't care who saw us. I didn't ever want to let go of her, and now, twenty years later, I never have.

But before all those years passed, another miracle happened. I was sixteen years old at the time. The folks had about twenty feeder calves on the farm, and I fed those calves their ground corn twice each day, yelling barnyard vulgarities at them as you have to do to make the big ones stop pushing the little ones away from the feedbunk. When yelling didn't work, I hit them with a stick. The stick didn't hurt them, but it held their attention for five or ten seconds. Then they started pushing the little calves again.

During the day, the calves went out to graze in one of the bluegrass pastures. At night, they slept wherever they wanted. But when winter came, I spread straw on the dirt floor of the barn every night so the calves could lie down and sleep while the collective heat from their bodies raised the temperature in the barn.

When summer arrived and the weather improved, I gave the farm the same treatment I gave it every year. I hitched the manure spreader to the tractor and parked it beside the door to the barn. Then I began doing what all cattle farmers used to do. Using a five-tine manure fork, I loaded the layers of straw and manure into the spreader until it was full. Then I drove the tractor out to the field, put the spreader in gear, and rode along the side of a hill as the spikes on the steel wheels at the back of the machine threw the nitrogen-rich mixture out to the rear.

Every once in a while, one of the rotating wheels didn't operate exactly right and tossed a clod of manure toward the front instead of the rear. Whenever one of those clods hit me in the back of the head, I said the sort of things that candidates for sainthood should never say.

Then one day I was driving the tractor along a hillside, looking back occasionally to see how the load was progressing. The machine was about half empty when I glanced back and saw something impossible. The steel wheels were catching the manure in the usual way and throwing out something transformed. Thousands of flower petals had flown from the back of the spreader and landed on the hillside, creating a magic pasture unlike anything that anyone had ever seen.

I stopped the tractor right there, turned off the engine, and climbed down. I wanted to make sure I wasn't hallucinating. The flower petals were everywhere the spreader had traveled on that hillside. They included every color I had ever imagined, and they were absolutely real. I picked one up and looked at it carefully. I could still tell the difference between a flower petal and a clod of manure, and this was a flower petal. I held onto it as I turned and walked back to the house.

I didn't have to convince the folks to go out to the field to have a look. "Lester," Mom shouted, "Michael's done it again."

Dad was out front, digging a posthole for the fence between our yard and the neighbor's pasture. "I always have to fix my fences and the neighbor's," he said as he came through the door. "I wish the old fool would let me buy those forty acres like I've been offering for years." The "old fool" in this case was a man who lived in Des Moines and never did anything with his land but rent it to a sheep farmer.

"Well, Michael," Dad said, "What miracle have you done this time? Now that we've become Catholics, we need a steady supply to increase your chances for sainthood."

I handed him the flower petal, which happened to be orange in color. Then I told him the history of that petal. "Well, well," he said. "It doesn't look like cow shit. How does it smell?" He put the petal under his nose and took a deep breath. "Doesn't smell like cow shit. Angie, we'd better go take a look at this. Looks like another money maker to me."

"I'll be damned," Dad said when he saw his flower-strewn hayfield. "What do you think, Angie?"

"I'll go in and call KTVO," she said. "Then I'll call Mary. It's almost four o'clock, and Floyd won't be fit to do much of anything this late in the afternoon, but he's probably still awake."

Aunt Mary drove them right over. Just to give them the full effect of the thing, I started the tractor and pulled the spreader about twenty yards. "Son of a bitch," Uncle Floyd said several times as he followed the manure spreader. "Better not try to bale this, Lester," he said.

"Floyd," Mom said, "why don't you put that six-pack back in the car and try to sober up for once in your life. We know enough not to bale a field of flower petals. Mary," she said, turning in Aunt Mary's direction, "I don't know how you put up with him."

"He gets a lot of work done in the morning," Aunt Mary said.

"All right, all right," Dad said. "Let's call off the AA meeting and decide what to do with this new miracle."

"KTVO said they'd send someone right over," Mom said, and fifteen minutes later, a van loaded with people and equipment came down the lane, leaving a trail of gravel dust behind it.

The station ran the story that night, and everything proceeded as it had with my water-walking act, with certain differences. Early every morning, Dad, Uncle Floyd, and I had to get up and load the manure spreader. If Uncle Floyd had brought any beer along, Mom took it away from him and hid it. Once the spreader was loaded, she returned the beer, which motivated Uncle Floyd to work faster.

Then there was another important difference between the two miracles. The number of people who arrived to see the show was much smaller. Mom said it was because of a Methodist boycott, but Dad said he hadn't seen all that many Catholics. The parking lot was only half the size of the previous one, and the folks had to hire only four off-duty cops to direct traffic and keep order. "You know what I think?" Aunt Mary said.

"What?" Mom said.

"People are stupid, and they've already seen one miracle. They think if they've seen one, they've seen them all. They'd rather stay at home and watch TV instead of coming out here to see another miracle performed by a boy destined for saint-hood."

Neither Mom nor Dad could think of anything to say about that. And the next morning, after only three weeks of business, the manure stopped turning into flower petals. From crap it came, and to crap it had returned.

When Katie and I were both eighteen, she got pregnant. And there was nothing immaculate about it. Father Rossi hurried things along for us. Katie was already a Catholic and didn't have to convert.

"Every birth is a miracle," Father Rossi told us, "and you don't have to walk on water to create a baby. Millions of people do it every year all over the world. And if your child grows into a healthy and happy adult, she'll be a saint. Love and care for your little miracle."

When I got home that afternoon, Aunt Mary and Uncle Floyd were there. I told everyone what Father Rossi had said. Mom, Dad, and Aunt Mary nodded in agreement.

"I don't believe a baby's a miracle," Uncle Floyd said. "It's just another baby."

"Shut up, Floyd," Mom said. "You're as drunk as always. If you're sober at your own funeral, it'll be a miracle."

PALERMO
COFFEE

When Mario Zuber looked at a photo of himself, he saw a champion of commerce, one of the thousands of heroes who kept the cash registers humming from Baltimore to Bakersfield. Mario made his living as a bookkeeper. Every day, Monday through Friday, he gathered the receipts, scribbled notes, and other records provided by his customers. Then he walked out of his apartment in the village of Albany and drove his old Chevy ten miles south to Carlville, a busy little town on the Maple River.

In the center of Carlville, Mario parked in front of the Palermo Coffee House, which occupied a building made from two-by-fours, particle board, and imitation bricks. On windy days, the shop creaked and moaned like a tired barn. Once inside, Mario seized a large table, ordered coffee, and got to work. For the next eight hours, he updated and reconciled the books for his clients. Along the way, he ordered just enough coffee to justify his residence at the table.

Because Mario kept the books for the coffee house, Angelo Bach, the owner, soon told him to sit wherever he chose. "Enjoy yourself while you work," Mr. Bach said. "And you can drink all the coffee you want at no charge."

"Thank you," Mario said in his gentle way. "You're very kind."

Mario worked at the Palermo Coffee House because its name reminded him of all the lovely places he'd never visited, places that had no need for snowplows. He hoped to live in Palermo or some other Mediterranean city after making his fortune, although he didn't know how many years that would take.

In order to speed things along, Mario began to relieve the Palermo Coffee House of more sugar, straws, and other commodities than he really needed. He collected silverware, plates, and cups. He walked out with bananas, apples, and oranges. His apartment contained a growing supply of artificial flowers, boxes of tea, and bags of potato chips. Once each week, he went home with a gallon of milk, forty-eight bagels, and a bucket of cream cheese. And because he drank so much coffee, he found ways to rescue toilet paper, soap, and paper towels during his frequent visits to the men's john.

Mr. Bach noticed that the shop was using more of these items than in the past, but this didn't seem to affect his cash flow. The books showed that he was doing fine, and Mario always kept such good records. Meanwhile, back in bucolic Albany, Mario began holding sidewalk sales every Saturday afternoon. Because his costs were zero, he sold everything at a discount and developed a regular clientele. "Mario," one lady said, "you always have such a nice variety goods."

"Thank you," Mario said. "I do my best."

Mr. Bach sometimes had to leave the shop to conduct business elsewhere. On one of those days, he said, "Mario, could you take care of the place until I get back?"

"Certainly," Mario said. "Don't worry about a thing." This arrangement soon became part of his daily routine, and on those occasions, money fell to earth from a merciful God. Mario found it easy to collect forty or fifty dollars by pocketing the money from only ten percent of the sales. Each morning, he brought along a cigar box filled with change and used it instead of the cash register for those transactions. "No records, no loss" became his motto.

But when even this didn't bring in money fast enough, Mario began to escalate his campaign. Two times a week, he went to a store owned by one of his other clients and set up there for a few hours. While working at a card table in the storage room of a small hardware store, he helped himself to nails, nuts, and bolts. On another day, hammers, flashlights, and power drills found their way out the back door and into the trunk of his car. At an entertainment store, Mario collected CDs, DVDs, and video games. Finally, after removing bird feeders, sprinklers, and flagstones from a yard and garden store, Mario realized he needed help.

He found it in the person of a young woman named Carlotta Ludwig, a perky blonde who had just graduated from the Carlville Community College and was eager to find a job. She proved to be an excellent bookkeeper, and Mario soon turned over much of his work to her, leaving him with only the most lucrative businesses to serve—places like those selling designer fashions, electronic hardware, or glass knickknacks that were both useless and expensive.

Mario made these acquisitions carefully, removing only one or two objects per month. His trophies included laptop computers, a 50-inch Toshiba television set with light-emitting diodes, and a late-model Mercedes-Benz worth $92,350. As Carlotta became more acquainted with the business, Mario introduced her to his most-rewarding ventures. "Always remember," he said, "as far as the records are concerned, products can't disappear from inventory if they were never added to inventory. And live simply so that you don't draw attention to yourself. Imitate Meyer Lansky, not Bernie Madoff."

As he grew older, Mario started to think about religion. He began to worship the Greco-Roman Gods and Goddesses of the ancient world, to which he added other gods of his own making. At the top of this celestial gathering, Mario installed Palermos, the God of Coffee Houses.

Mario had also become an important member of the local community. He joined the Chamber of Commerce, the Better Business Bureau, and the United Way. He solicited contributions for the Salvation Army. He collected toys and clothing for needy children. He gathered contributions for the victims of natural disasters. He advocated better academic programs to educate future legions of bookkeepers. Ultimately, as one might've predicted, he received the prestigious Carlville Community Betterment Award. During an emotional acceptance speech, Mario said, "I've never felt more loved and more needed."

One week later, fire destroyed Mario's apartment. When they heard the news, hundreds of people rushed to his aid. Luckily, he'd insured all the expensive furniture, appliances, and electronic equipment lost in what the fire marshal said was an unusually hot fire.

A week after the fire, having toiled for thirty years, Mario sold his entire business to Carlotta Ludwig, who promised to continue running it in a thoroughly professional way.

◉ ◉ ◉

Mario Zuber died in Palermo, Sicily, at the age of sixty-four. He'd just visited a number of stores in the city and was returning to his villa when he fell down a flight of stairs and cracked his skull on a marble balustrade. The medical examiner noted that Mario had four rolls of toilet paper and a nice set of silverware in the pockets of his raincoat. As Mario had previously requested, a mortician transported his body to a crematorium and later spread his ashes on the warm waters of the Tyrrhenian Sea.

THE LILY
OF THE
WEST

Jim Parker brought two things home from the Korean War, a Purple Heart and an addiction to whiskey. With these additions to his résumé, he returned to his eighty-acre farm, which stood at the end of a gravel lane in southern Iowa. When Charlie and Flora Nolan moved into the farmhouse at the other end of the lane, Parker caught glimpses of both husband and wife, but only the image of the wife aroused his interest.

The fence that separated his lane from the Nolan place had become cluttered with saplings and young trees during the war, and when the leaves came out in the spring, they obscured Parker's view of Nolan's house, Nolan's barn, and Nolan's wife. Parker often wished he had a wife of his own, but no one wanted to marry a drunk, with or without a Purple Heart.

If Parker wanted a better view of Nolan's wife, he'd have to cut down the trees and saplings, which was something he'd put off doing until some unknown time in the future. But this time, he searched everywhere until he found his double-bladed ax. With the ax in his right hand, he headed toward the lane in work shoes, a pair of jeans, a T-shirt, and a straw hat with the brim turned up on both sides like a Hollywood cowboy's.

Parker went straight to work. The weather was warm, and he started to sweat. He took off his T-shirt and displayed a torso that God had given to him and certain other young men, such as Sugar Ray Robinson, Ted Williams, and Michelangelo's *David*. Parker was sure that if Flora Nolan saw him working at that moment, she'd see something worth looking at.

The next Saturday afternoon, while Parker was turning the saplings into sawdust, Charlie Nolan walked down the lane to say hello, but Flora didn't come with him. Parker and Nolan talked about the price of beef cattle, the lack of rain, and Morrell's Packinghouse in Ottumwa. Parker had found a job there, and Nolan needed one, too. Parker said the managers were idiots and that Nolan should tell the man who did the hiring that he never wanted to join the union. A convincing lie might get him a job. Nolan said thanks for the advice and walked back down the lane.

After working at the packinghouse all day, Parker usually arrived home about four o'clock. His first task was to get the stink off himself by removing his slaughterhouse clothes, taking a shower, and putting on his beef-farmer clothes. Then he drank two large glasses of bourbon and went out to feed the calves their ground corn, spreading it in a feedbunk that Parker himself had made in high-school shop class. Parker liked his calves, and they liked him. He'd raised them from youngsters, and they were all best friends. The calves would eventually pay the ultimate price for Parker's bourbon, but he tried not to think about that.

One Tuesday afternoon, as Parker arrived home after work, he caught a glimpse of Flora Nolan. She was working in the garden between her house and Parker's lane, and she'd dressed for the job. She wore sneakers, a sleeveless blouse with a neckline that plunged to record depths, and a pair of shorts just long enough to meet the requirements of state laws and local ordinances. Parker drove his blue Pontiac past this spectacle as slowly as low gear would allow. He noticed Flora's dark-brown hair, which looked good with her red blouse. The Pontiac's eight cylinders could not inhale and exhale any slower than what they were already doing, so Parker couldn't make a closer examination. But he did suddenly understand the importance of gardening.

That same afternoon—after the shower, the change of clothes, the two glasses of bourbon, and the corn for the calves—Parker went to the tool shed to get the ax. The job couldn't wait until the weekend. Saplings were the deadly enemies of woven-wire fences and their two strands of barbed wire at the top. Parker had inherited his eighty-acre farm at a time when farmers still understood that a healthy man could complete a simple job without buying expensive tools. He didn't need a power saw, the cost of which would devastate his whiskey budget. Besides that, the bourbon made him feel invincible, just as it had in Korea.

The saplings and small trees began falling under the strength of Parker's powerful arms, legs, and torso—each one revealing a better view of Flora Nolan, a revelation far more compelling than any that Parker had ever found in the Bible. Before her early death, Parker's mother had tried to make him read the most common Bible stories, but he never got interested in people who ate endless amounts of fish while wandering across deserts and over rock piles.

Parker had chopped his way about a fourth of the distance from his house to the Nolan garden when his superhuman strength began to feel more like conventional human weakness. Leaving the ax behind, Parker walked back to the house, where he constructed and demolished three ham sandwiches.

He followed this with two more large glasses of bourbon, then lay down on the couch to rest his back before returning to the saplings. But he didn't return to the saplings at all that afternoon. Instead, he fell asleep and awoke the next morning at five o'clock.

◉ ◉ ◉

Parker spent several minutes figuring out who he was, where he was, and what to do next. Having solved these mysteries, he put on his packinghouse clothes, fed the calves, ate six scrambled eggs with six strips of bacon and six pieces of toast, and drank an unknown amount of black coffee. Then he drove the Pontiac twenty miles north on Route 63 to John Morrell and Company in Ottumwa.

As always happened, the stench of the plant drove what remained of his hangover out of his head. At seven o'clock, he and the other men working with him began carrying frozen beef quarters out of the plant and into the refrigerated boxcars of the Chicago, Burlington & Quincy Railroad. The CB&Q would pull the cars east to Chicago, where another railroad would take them the rest of the way to New York City. The job of loading these cars required men who were big, strong, and able to carry heavy loads. And they had to do it all day long.

The only thing Parker didn't like about the job was the foreman, who seemed to spend all his time thinking of ways to criticize his workers, especially Parker. "Try moving a little faster, Parker," he said.

"I'm moving as fast as the other guys," Parker said. "I can't jump over them."

"You're the one slowing everyone else down."

Parker made no response to this lie. Instead, he entertained a fantasy in which he picked up the foreman, carried him into the car, and hung him on one of the hooks for a chilly ride to New York.

◉ ◉ ◉

A few months later, as Parker lay in his coffin at Hopewell Cemetery after his funeral, he remembered the foreman, the saplings along the lane, and Flora. He wondered what all the other people were thinking about in their coffins. He knew who was lying next to him—his parents and his brother. "Hello, Mom. Hello, Pop," he said.

"No talking until after sundown," his mother said.

"Okay," Parker said. "How will I know when it's sundown?"

"Everyone will start talking."

"How you doing, Jimmy?" Willie said.

"Just fine, Willie," Parker answered, "except for this hole in my head."

"Willie, no talking," Mom said.

"I just wanted to say hello to Jimmy."

"Willie, do as your mother says," Pop said.

Willie stopped talking. Parker got the idea and became as silent as the grave. "As silent as the grave" is an expression that's always used by people who've never been in a grave, but Parker soon learned that there's so much chatter in a graveyard after sundown that you can't get to sleep until two or three o'clock in the morning.

Parker remained quiet the rest of the afternoon, spending his time thinking about Flora. After he'd finished clearing the fence line of its saplings and young trees—and their offending leaves—he fell into the habit of observing Flora through a pair of powerful binoculars that he'd paid for by switching to an inferior brand of bourbon for several weeks. The binoculars turned out to be worth the sacrifice, because Flora always seemed to do her gardening after Parker got home from work.

Allowing himself all the time he needed, Parker inventoried Flora's features. Her ankles were slim and well formed. The act of walking accented the curves of her calves and thighs. Her waist and breasts, when viewed through Parker's binoculars, were slim in the first case and prominent in the second. Her hair was long and dark brown. She had a dark complexion by Fox County standards, and Parker wondered if she was a Mexican. He couldn't be sure about the color of her eyes, but he thought they matched the color of her hair. The binoculars proved one thing for sure. Her face had all the symmetry we normally associate with beauty.

Parker soon noticed that Flora's husband never seemed to be around when it was time to adjust the binoculars. A visit to the Farmers' Tavern in Clearfield elicited the information that Nolan had obtained a job with the cleanup crew at the packinghouse. Just as Parker left work every afternoon, Nolan and his comrades were advancing with their hoses, brushes, soap, and disinfectants to remove all the blood, mud, and shit that polluted the inside of the huge plant.

Cleanup was a crap job, but so were all the other jobs at the slaughterhouse. The advantage was that the people who worked at night got paid extra, while everyone else was at home watching *I Love Lucy*, or, as in Parker's case, watching his neighbor's wife.

The day after he learned about Nolan's new job at Morrell's, Parker found it convenient to forget to collect the mail from the mailbox when he reached his lane after work. If a man's going to forget his mail, he needs to do it early in the growing season, before his neighbor's wife has no more work to do in the garden.

"Jimmy," Willie said, interrupting Parker's recollections, "Is it really true about you and Flora Nolan? We've heard a lot of stories."

This question posed a moral and theological problem for Parker. Here he was, lying in the grave, while the higher authorities were trying to decide what to do with his immortal soul. If he told Willie the stories were true, that would reinforce certain charges against him. If he said the stories were false, certain authorities might raise charges of lying against him. Did he really want to say something that might be a lie while he was already in the grave? He hesitated until Mom said, "Willie, no talking."

In the silence that followed, Parker remembered the day he forgot the mail. After taking off his packinghouse clothes, he took a shower, put on his beef-farmer clothes, drank two large glasses of bourbon, and forgot to feed the calves.

He walked down the lane to the mailbox with nothing more than a glance at Flora, who was murdering every weed that had crept into her perfect rows of flowers and vegetables. Her vegetables included tomatoes, green beans, spinach, and many others. But all her flowers were lilies, the whitest lilies anyone had ever seen in Fox County.

Parker retrieved his mail, pretended to look at it, walked back down the lane ten or fifteen yards, and stopped just across the fence from Flora. Simultaneously, she stopped using the hoe, stood up straight, and looked at him.

Without a word, both of them smiled, thereby revealing that both had perfect teeth. And at this distance, Parker saw that Flora had coal-black eyes. He couldn't read her mind, but the likelihood was that his appearance was as attractive to her as hers was to him—his strong body, his wavy brown hair, and his eyes the color of the bluest robin eggs ever seen.

"Would you like something to drink?" Flora said.

Parker said he would. In the kitchen, he saw that everything was as tidy and well organized as Flora's garden. Beside a window that afforded a view of Parker's lane, house, and barn, an expensive pair of binoculars lay on a counter. "What would you like?" Flora said. "We have ice tea, beer, and a bottle of bourbon."

Flora drank ice tea. Parker drank bourbon. After the drinks, they stood there silently awhile. "Are you Mexican," Parker said.

"No, I'm German," Flora said. Then she took his hand and led him into the bedroom.

It was dark by the time Parker returned home. The calves were upset about the change in their normal routine. They didn't care how much fun Parker had been having with the neighbor's wife. They wanted their supper. Parker stumbled about in the darkness, making apologies as he spread the corn in the feedbunk. "Sorry, boys, sorry," he said.

As always, the big calves tried to push the little ones away from the feedbunk. "Here now, here now," Parker said, using the same words and inflections his father had used with his livestock.

After the calves had recovered their calf-like bliss, Parker went into the house, turned on the TV news, and paid no attention to it. He was too much in love to care about local events. He didn't drink any more bourbon. He just floated here and there in a dream world where Flora Nolan was the only other human being alive. Foremen, husbands, and other troubling presences disappeared.

At midnight, he undressed and fell into bed. Just as he was drifting toward sleep, he remembered something—the mail. He'd left it beside the binoculars on Flora's kitchen counter.

Parker did not get a good night's sleep. He spent a great deal of time trying to think of a believable explanation for how his mail came to be resting beside Flora's binoculars on the kitchen counter in Nolan's house. Nolan would be home by now, so Parker couldn't just call Flora and tell her to hide the mail. Nolan might answer the phone, and he wouldn't be receptive to anything other than the obvious reason for the pile of mail, all clearly addressed to Parker. Nor could Parker knock on the Nolan door just to make a neighborly midnight visit.

When it came to the Ten Commandments, most of the people in Fox County were strict constructionists. Sexual congress with your neighbor's wife would not win their sympathy, and many would look the other way if Nolan got out his deer rifle, attached the scope, and filled Parker's vital organs with .30-caliber holes.

This image of an armed and angry Nolan prompted Parker to get *his* deer rifle out of the closet. He would defend his eighty acres at all cost. He was, after all, a highly trained infantryman. He'd fought in many battles in Korea, although there was no evidence that his bullets had ever hit any of the opposing soldiers, which was commonplace for infantrymen who went into battle while intoxicated.

Parker loaded the rifle, locked all the doors and windows, and turned out the lights. In the darkness, he pushed the couch over against the front door. Next he turned the kitchen table on its side and pushed it up against the couch. He needed sand-bags, but none was available. So he and the rifle lay down on the floor. No one could see him there, and this would give him an advantage if a battle broke out.

Parker turned this way and that most of the night. At four-thirty, he fell asleep. At five-thirty, the alarm woke him up. He lay there a few minutes, thinking about the prospect of carrying beef quarters all day on only one hour's sleep. But fear of desti-tution pushed him out of his bunker.

After drinking several cups of coffee, he put on his slaugh-terhouse clothes, fed the calves, ate breakfast, and packed his lunch. While doing all this, he kept the rifle close at hand, just in case Nolan launched an early morning attack. Finally, he put the rifle back into the closet, locked the door to the house, and walked out to his Pontiac. Even though he realized that no one in Fox County knew how to construct a car bomb, he searched for one anyway. Then he looked across the fields and trees at the clock on the north side of the bell tower of the Fox County Courthouse. The clock said six-thirty, which matched the time on his wristwatch. He got into the car, started the engine, and drove to the packinghouse.

⊙ ⊙ ⊙

"What about Flora Nolan?" Willie said. "Did you really do you-know-what with her?"

"Willie, I don't want to talk about it. I might say something to incriminate myself. Besides, I don't know if it's all right for us to talk yet."

"It's all right," Mom said. "Start talking."

"Just a minute," Pop said. "Everyone in this graveyard can hear what Jimmy says. Some things are better left unsaid."

"We'll whisper," Willie said.

"That doesn't work here, and you know it," Pop said.

That ended the discussion, but it reminded Parker of that sleepless night and the long day that followed. As usual, Nolan had left for work by the time Parker drove back down his lane that afternoon. Parker was feeding the calves when Flora walked down the lane and across the lawn to the barn lot. She leaned against a fence post and said, "Hi, cowboy." Parker wasn't expecting her, and her greeting startled him.

"Flora," he said, "you scared me."

"You don't have to be scared of me," she said. "I just walked down the lane to deliver your mail. You left it in my kitchen last night."

"I know," he said, trying not to show his embarrassment. "Did Charlie find it?"

"No, I found it. It may feel a little cool to you. I hid it under the pork chops in the deepfreeze."

"Thank God," Parker said. "I worried about it all night."

"Poor baby," she said. "You are my baby, aren't you?"

Parker felt a surge of hormones. "Yes," he said, "I'm your baby."

Parker usually groomed the calves with a curry comb after feeding them in the afternoon. But he skipped it that day. Instead, he and Flora walked across the lawn and into the house. He asked her to wait while he changed the sheets on the bed, but Flora was eager. She helped with the sheets.

These visits quickly became a routine. It was safer to meet at Parker's house than at Flora's. He didn't have to worry about leaving the mail in Flora's kitchen. She didn't have to fuss with the pork chops in the deepfreeze.

They talked about what they might and might not do in the future. They weren't in a hurry. Then one day, the routine ended. Flora didn't come down the lane to watch Parker feed the calves. He called her telephone number, but she didn't answer. He walked down the lane and knocked on her door, but she didn't open it and invite him in. He repeated all this for days, but she was never home. She became his missing person. But he couldn't ask Nolan about her without arousing suspicion.

She was gone, vanished. Parker saw Nolan once in a while, sometimes in town, sometimes when Nolan was working on his farm. Nolan always smiled and waved, as if Parker were his best friend. Then Flora's garden disappeared, replaced by a carpet of bluegrass. "How could this happen?" Parker wondered. But he didn't see how he could call the sheriff to report a missing garden.

Parker had never felt so miserable. He found all sorts of jobs that needed to be done on the farm. Work helped him forget about Flora for a while. There were always saplings along the fence rows. One Saturday, he took the ax and walked to a hilltop near the back of the farm. It was about ninety-five degrees, and he began to sweat. He took off his T-shirt and dropped it beside the water jug. Then he looked down the hill toward the property line between his place and Ernie Young's. Ernie was an old man by then, and Parker rarely saw him, although he often heard him calling his milk cows late in the afternoon. Ernie still had a powerful voice.

A patch of timber stood on the side of the hill. Parker and his father had always left this timber alone. It provided shade for whatever kind of livestock they owned. Just in front of the woods, blackberry bushes offered berries to anyone energetic enough to pick them. Parker felt no need for blackberries at the moment. The saplings required his attention.

He picked up the water jug, took a long drink, and set it down. He looked toward the woods again and saw a woman dressed all in white—white dress, white gloves, and a white hat. She picked some berries and dropped them into a basket. Then she stopped and turned to the side, giving Parker a view of her face. It was Flora, who had once grown the whitest lilies in Fox County, but her image seemed indistinct, almost transparent.

He started down the hill just as she disappeared into the woods. He knew he'd find her. The patch of timber was small.

He couldn't miss her. He ran through the trees all the way to the fence. Beyond it, Ernie Young's hayfield covered the narrow valley. No one was there. And no one was in the woods. Parker had lost her, lost her forever, his Flora, the lily of the west.

NEW MONEY

"Hey, kid," said the man on the park bench, "wanna make some money?"

Danny looked at the man cautiously. His mother had told him to be careful around strangers. But she had also told him that someday he'd be old enough to earn money for the family. Maybe he was old enough now. "What do I have to do?" he said, keeping his distance.

"It's easy, real easy." The man had short brown hair and a round face. He wore a baggy suit, but no tie. "See this twenty-dollar bill?" he said. "You just take it and buy something—anything you want, just as long as it doesn't cost over five dollars.

Then you bring me back fifteen dollars in change, and you keep whatever you bought and any money that's left over."

"I can buy anything I want?"

"Sure, anything you want."

"And all I have to do is to give you back fifteen dollars?"

"That's it. See, I told you it was easy." He held out the twenty-dollar bill. "What do you say?" Danny hesitated. "Come on, come on, it won't hurt you. You'll never find an easier job than this."

Danny inched forward, took the money, and backed away quickly.

"There," the man said. "That wasn't so bad, was it? Bring me back fifteen dollars, and I'll let you do it again. Just don't tell anyone where you got the money. Okay?"

"Okay," Danny said. He walked out of the park and stopped on the sidewalk to inspect the twenty-dollar bill. It looked brand new. It was as clean as his mother's best tablecloth, and it didn't have a crease in it.

He put the money into the pocket of his jeans and walked down the street to an ice-cream store. "Danny, what can I get you today?" said the middle-aged woman behind the counter.

"A small chocolate shake," Danny said. He would've bought a large one, but he didn't want to pay the extra price.

The woman made the milkshake and set it on the counter. "That'll be two dollars," she said. Danny took out the twenty and handed it to her. She rang up the sale and put the money into the cash drawer. "Here you go, big boy," she said, giving him his change. Danny was eight years old, but his baby face sometimes caused adults to treat him like a toddler.

He sat down at a small round table and counted the money. He had fifteen dollars for the man in the park and three dollars for himself. This really was an easy way to make money.

He polished off the milkshake, then walked back to the park. The man was still sitting on the same bench. "How'd it go?" he said.

"Just fine," Danny said.

"You got my fifteen dollars?" Danny handed him the money. "Good boy," the man said. "You wanna do it again?"

"Sure." Danny couldn't wait to see how surprised his mom would be when he gave her all that money.

"Here's another twenty for you."

Danny took the twenty-dollar bill. Like the first one, it was brand new. He looked at the picture on the back. The bushes in front of the White House were as green as the ones in the park.

"There's just one thing," the man said. "Don't go back to the same place. Never go to the same place more than once a day."

"Are we going to do this again tomorrow?" Danny said.

"You bet. This is an important job."

Danny walked out of the park and down the street to another ice-cream store, where he bought another small chocolate milkshake. Halfway through it, he began to feel stuffed. He left the unfinished portion behind and went back to the park.

"Ready to go again?" the man asked after pocketing his fifteen dollars.

"I don't think so," Danny said. "I have to go home. But I'll come back tomorrow after school if you want me to."

"Sure. You bet. You run on home, and I'll see you back here again tomorrow. And remember, don't tell anyone where you got the money."

As Danny walked away, he looked back over his shoulder. The man was handing a twenty-dollar bill to another boy.

⊚ ⊚ ⊚

"Danny, where'd you get all that money?" his mother said after he handed her six one-dollar bills. She had just got home and was still wearing her white uniform. Lucy, Danny's four-year-old sister, coaxed the money out of her mother's hand and began playing with it on the floor.

"At the bus depot," Danny said, "carrying people's things for them." He didn't want to lie to his mother, but the man had said not to tell.

"I'm glad to have it, Danny, but I'm not sure I want you hanging around that bus depot." Danny's sister jumped up and ran into the apartment's only bedroom.

"It's okay, Mom. There's a policeman right there all the time." His mother stood with a hand on her cheek. Her skin was as fair as Lucy's, her hair as dark, her eyes as blue. "A big policeman," Danny added. His sister ran back into the room with her panda bear and began teaching it how to count money.

"Well, I suppose it's all right if there's a policeman there. But be careful, Danny. And thank you for the money." She bent down and hugged him.

⊚ ⊚ ⊚

The next day, Danny went back to the park right after school. "Remember," said the man on the park bench, "don't go to the same place more than once a day, and don't tell anyone where you got the money. I don't want anyone stealing it."

For his first stop of the afternoon, Danny selected a large drugstore, where he bought four pencils and a large eraser. While walking back to the park, he thought about just how easy this job was. In fact, it was too easy. The man was handing out money for almost nothing in return. If he wanted change for his twenty-dollar bills, why didn't he buy things for himself and keep all the change? Danny decided to ask.

"That's a good question," the man said after taking his fifteen dollars, "a real good question. You see, I work for the government, and it's my job to put new money into circulation and take the old money out of circulation. Otherwise, all the money that people use would wear out, and they wouldn't have anything to buy stuff with. You see what I mean?"

"Yes," Danny said.

"So, you see, this is a real important job, and I need all the help I can get. If it wasn't for people like you and me, the stores would all go out of business. The whole country would just fall apart."

With this explanation in mind, Danny worked until almost five o'clock. Altogether, he put eighty dollars' worth of new money into circulation, saving four businesses from the danger of old money.

When he got home, Danny gave Lucy four new pencils, a large eraser, and a package of stickers. He gave his mother a new comb, a quart of milk, and twelve dollars in cash. "My word," his mother said, "are you sure you're not working too hard at that bus depot?"

"Don't worry, Mom," he said. "It's easy, just like helping you carry the groceries."

⊚ ⊚ ⊚

For the next two weeks, Danny went to the park every day right after school. When he arrived a little past three o'clock, the man was always waiting on the same park bench. Two older boys also worked for the man. Like Danny, they usually went home around four-thirty or five.

Then one day, school let out an hour early. When Danny reached the edge of the park, he saw the man walking into the woods behind the bench where he usually sat. Danny walked over to the bench and waited a couple of minutes. When the man didn't come back, Danny went into the woods to find him.

He was walking quietly through the trees when he heard a noise. He crept forward and peeked around a tree. The man was kneeling on the ground, but he wasn't praying. He was pulling a canvas bag out of a hollow log. Something made Danny wish he hadn't followed him into the woods.

The man reached into the canvas bag, took out a handful of new money, and shoved the bag back into the log. Then he put the money into one of his pockets and walked out of the woods.

Danny didn't want the man to think he was spying on him. So he waited until he was out of earshot, then left the woods by a different route. After going halfway around the park, he walked over to the man's bench from the usual direction.

"You're early today," the man said cheerfully.

"They let us out early," Danny said. "The teachers are having a meeting."

"That's good. That'll give you more time to work, won't it?"

"Uh-huh." Danny looked at the man for a moment. "Do you keep your money in a bank?" he said.

"A bank? Oh, no. I wouldn't put it in a bank. Banks aren't safe. It's too easy to rob them. I hide all the money I use where no one can find it. That's what you have to do when you work for the government." He handed Danny his first twenty-dollar bill of the day. "Stay away from banks," he said. "You never know what's gonna happen in a place like that."

◉ ◉ ◉

Every day, Monday through Friday, Danny brought some money home for his mother. In addition to that, he brought something home for his sister—things such as crayons, stickers, or coloring books. It was an agreeable routine, and everyone came to expect it.

Then one afternoon, Danny arrived at the park and the man wasn't there. He thought about looking in the woods, but he didn't want to find any more secrets. The two older boys arrived and stood around for a while. But they soon grew impatient and took off in opposite directions.

Danny stayed until almost five, then walked home. He told his sister and his mother that all the people at the bus depot had wanted to carry their own things that day. Lucy moaned and said, "Not fair!" Then she turned and stomped away, her ponytail bouncing with each step.

His mother put her hand on her cheek and looked at him. "That's strange," she said, "after all the other times." Danny didn't try to explain.

He went back to the park again the next afternoon, but the man was nowhere in sight. Neither were the other two boys. Danny waited an hour before leaving. When he got home, he said that not many people were riding the buses that day. Lucy said, "Stupid people!"

His mother stood there with a look of uncertainty on her face. "Danny," she said, "you're not doing anything to get in trouble, are you? You know I can't follow you around all day."

"No, Mom," he said. "I'm not getting in trouble."

The next day was Saturday. That morning, as he was playing on the sidewalk, Danny saw one of the two older boys riding down the street on his bicycle. He ran out to the curb to stop him. "What do you want?" the boy said. He had reached the age when talking to younger children was viewed as a great burden.

"What happened to the man with the new money?" Danny said.

"You mean you don't know?"

"No."

"They sent him back for parole violation."

"Oh." Danny had no idea what "parole violation" meant.

"Yeah, possession of something or other."

"When's he coming back?"

"Not for a long time."

"How long?"

"I don't know. Not for a long, long time." He put his right foot on the bicycle pedal. "They say he's working in the laundry." The boy laughed and took off on his bike. Danny watched him until he disappeared around the corner a block away.

⊙ ⊙ ⊙

After school the following Monday, Danny hurried out the door and walked straight to the park. He stopped beside the familiar bench and looked around. There was no one in sight. He walked into the woods.

He'd thought about it all weekend, ever since talking to the boy on Saturday. His mother needed money. He needed chocolate shakes. And his sister needed all kinds of stuff.

Besides that, it was his duty. He didn't know when the man would come back, but people had to buy things right now. He couldn't just let all the money in town wear out.

He stopped beside the hollow log and got down on his hands and knees. He reached inside, grabbed the canvas bag, and pulled. It wasn't easy. The bag was stuffed with money, new money, enough to last for years.

With four twenty-dollar bills in his pocket, Danny pushed the bag back into the log and walked out of the woods. There was still no one around. He stopped beside the park bench and surveyed the flowers, the bushes, and the blue sky. It looked like a two-shake afternoon. He walked out of the park, stopped at the first ice-cream store, and went to work.

THE

TRIFECTA

Zimbo walked into Cobalt Brokers at five-thirty in the afternoon. The office was small but seldom crowded—with recessed lighting, uncomfortable chairs, and a reception desk made of fiberglass and plastic. The desk held a large black console covered with glowing buttons that no one ever pushed.

Maria Sanchez, the receptionist, had dark-brown hair, dark-brown eyes, and a face beautiful enough to sink New Jersey. She'd been born in Puerto Rico, but grew up in Omaha, and Zimbo loved her more than any other woman in the history of the world. Cleopatra was okay for her time and place, as was Helen of Troy, but they came nowhere close to Maria.

Zimbo had brown hair and brown eyes like Maria's, but all the mirrors in Omaha told him he wasn't very good looking. A girl in junior high had once said he was cute, but that claim had never been independently verified.

"Hi, Zimbo," Maria said.

"Hello, Maria," he said. "Is the big guy here?"

Maria picked up the phone and punched in the appropriate numbers. In a cubicle ten feet behind her desk, a phone rang. After asking a series of questions, Maria said, "You're in luck, Zimbo. No one else is hiding back there. Go on in."

Julian Bradstreet was above average in height and circumference. He displayed a revolting smile and impossibly white teeth. His ensemble for the day included one of the many expensive suits Zimbo had seen him wearing. This particular suit was dark blue with red pinstripes. He wore a spotless white shirt and a red tie that matched the red pinstripes of his suit.

By way of contrast, Zimbo's business attire included one of his two pairs of pants, both of which were made of khaki-colored cotton and polyester. He wore one of his three shirts, each of which was different in color, this one being blue. He could not have worn a tie of any description because he didn't own one.

Bradstreet gave Zimbo a firm handshake, and they sat down. "What can I do for you today?" he said.

"I have fifty dollars," Zimbo said. "What can I buy with it?"

"Zimbo, with fifty dollars, you can buy one share of Interactive Prisons. Looks like a breakout stock to me." He laughed loudly at his own joke and reached over to give Zimbo's shirt sleeve a brotherly tug.

"I've never heard of it."

"That's because it just went public. The IPO jumped sixty percent the first day. I wish you'd called me last week."

"I can't afford a telephone, and I can't use the one at work for personal calls."

"Well, anyway, it's all part of the movement to privatize the country's prisons. It's going to make a lot of people rich. Are you sure you don't have more than fifty dollars?"

"I'm sure. My wife kept all the money when she kicked me out. I've got another seventy-five bucks, but I have to buy food for the rest of the month."

"Zimbo, the way this stock is heading, you'll have a small fortune before the month ends. You don't want to miss an opportunity like that, do you?"

"I suppose I could kick in another fifty if you really think this stock will take off."

"That's the spirit, Zimbo. And, as a matter of fact, it already took off."

Zimbo took the money out of his wallet and handed it over, pausing only to look at the twenty-five dollars he had left. "There you go," he said.

"Thanks a bunch," Bradstreet said as he picked up the telephone and called Maria, who was still only ten feet away. "Maria," he said, "could you give Zimbo a receipt for a hundred dollars."

"Sure thing," she said.

"I'll jump right on this, Zimbo," he said. "Don't worry about a thing."

"I'll try not to."

Bradstreet stuffed the money into an envelope labeled "Zimbo—IP." Then he tossed the envelope into a plastic basket on his desk. "Anything else I can do for you today?" he said.

"Yeah, I've been looking up stock-market websites on the computers at the library. What's a PE ratio?"

"It's complicated, Zimbo. Don't worry about it."

◉ ◉ ◉

The next day, Zimbo spent eight hours talking on the telephone to people who were angry about the fact that their insurance premiums had gone up. Many of these people expressed their desire to visit Omaha and dynamite the headquarters of the Trifecta Insurance Company, which occupied the Trifecta Tower, a pile of glass on Farnam Street. Zimbo thought the building was so ugly that it deserved demolition, but he kept that opinion to himself.

"I understand," he said to an irate woman in Colorado. "You could destroy the building, but that wouldn't reduce your premiums. Those premiums are based on your own driving history and the accident statistics for your town." Zimbo recited this speech word-for-word because that's what his boss had taught him to say. He actually had no idea how the premiums were set, and he had no idea how to sooth the angry caller. His boss hadn't taught him that.

"Idiot," the woman screamed. "I live in a town with fifty people. The only accident I ever had was pregnancy. And you just lost a customer." She slammed the phone down so hard that it sounded like the explosion she'd threatened to set off.

Zimbo sat there for a moment, waiting for the dynamite that would end his life. At the same moment, Alice Turly, Zimbo's boss, stopped at his cubicle and said, "Zimbo, your phone's ringing. What're you waiting for—Christmas? Hanukkah? Druidic Leap Year? Let's get moving, cowboy."

Zimbo felt a compelling need to throw Alice Turly into an angry volcano, but there were no volcanoes anywhere near Omaha. So he picked up the telephone and took another call.

After work, Zimbo walked to his apartment, which occupied the attic of an old frame house several blocks from downtown Omaha. He climbed two flights of stairs to reach his flat, in which the building's hipped roof caused the ceilings to slant down on all four sides. This created a hazard for anyone over five feet tall. Zimbo was five-six, and before he learned how to take evasive action, he'd raised lumps on his head while in the kitchen, the bathroom, the bedroom, and the living room—the entire apartment.

A dormer in the living room afforded the apartment its only two windows, which provided a view of abandoned factories and warehouses in the distance. Those windows also opened onto the fire escape, which the builder had not erected with great care, thereby creating a second hazard. Faced with two life-threatening dangers, Zimbo would have sold himself some life insurance, but he couldn't afford it.

The landlady had told him to buy some apartment insurance, but Zimbo couldn't afford that either and had ignored those instructions. He also couldn't afford a car, so he needed no auto insurance. He walked almost everywhere he went, except when he returned to Chicago to review the latest incidents of municipal graft and corruption. On those occasions, he called his sister Phyllis, who drove him to the Omaha Amtrak Station, complaining about the inconvenience all the way, "Why don't you buy a used car?" she always said.

"Can't afford it," Zimbo said.

"Why don't you call a cab?"

"Can't afford that either."

"If you didn't throw your money away on the stock market, you could afford all kinds of things."

"I'm creating wealth for my old age so I won't become a burden to society."

"Fat chance, Zimbo, fat chance. You'll lose everthing."

⊚ ⊚ ⊚

During his lunch break the next day, Zimbo walked over to Douglas Street and into the office of Cobalt Brokers. He wanted to see how his well-diversified portfolio of three stocks was doing. Maria went through her normal routine, first calling Julian Bradstreet, then telling Zimbo he'd have to wait a couple of minutes because another gentleman was conferring with the broker.

Zimbo put the time to good use by inviting Maria to come over to his apartment that night for spaghetti. "Zimbo," she said, "I simply love your spaghetti, but my mother said I should invite you to our house for dinner."

Zimbo salivated. "When and what time?" he said.

"How about tonight at seven o'clock?"

"I'll be there. Your mother's a great cook."

"Yes she is," Maria said, "and she taught me everything I need to know about cooking."

"Oh, I know," Zimbo said quickly.

"Not that cooking is the most important thing for a woman to learn."

"No, of course not," Zimbo said.

Zimbo would have continued agreeing with everything Maria said all day, but the conversation suddenly ended when a man emerged from Bradstreet's cubicle and walked out the door. Maria told Zimbo to go on back to the great man's desk, which he promptly did.

After effusive greetings, Bradstreet turned toward his computer, typed in a magic word, hit the "Enter" key, and waited as the page loaded. "You're having a great day," he said. "Interactive Prisons is up five percent. Late-Date Liquidators is up seven percent. And International Casinos is up ten percent. You can't do much better than that, Zimbo."

"That's good," Zimbo said, "but you know what?"

"What?"

"Some brokers have websites where their customers can look up their stocks. Then they can buy and sell shares without having to bother their brokers or pay an extra fee when the broker buys or sells for them."

"That's right, Zimbo. But Cobalt is a mega-discount brokerage. As you know, we charge only three dollars a trade and the broker places it for you. We couldn't offer extra services and still keep our fees so low. See what I mean?"

"I guess so."

"And one other thing, Zimbo."

"What?"

"When you come to see me, you're not bothering me. I'm here to help you. That's my job, Zimbo. That's my job." He paused. "See what I mean?"

"I see what you mean."

"Good. You still planning to add another position on payday?"

"I hope so."

"Good, Zimbo, good. Anything else I can do for you today?"

"Yeah. I looked up more stuff at the library the other day. What's a market cap?"

"It's complicated, Zimbo. Don't worry about it."

◉ ◉ ◉

Zimbo's afternoon at the Trifecta Insurance Company did not go well. Despite his efforts to placate angry customers, he had to cancel ten policies and survive nine dynamite threats. Then he had to endure his boss, Alice Turly, who never missed the slightest piece of bad news in the customer service department. She appeared to be on a mission from God, separating the wheat from the chaff, and Zimbo clearly belonged in the chaff hopper.

Just as he was preparing to leave at five o'clock, Ms. Turly materialized and blocked his escape. For that day's tribulations, she had adorned herself in a green business suit. "You know what, Zimbo?" she said.

"No, what?" Zimbo took a deep breath. His boss always reminded him of the women wrestlers on TV, with plenty of muscle and no charm.

"The mission of the customer service department is to help our clients and retain their business. It's not our mission to make them angry and lose their business."

"Yes," Zimbo said in agreement, wondering if Ms. Turly was about to give him a body slam or an elevated gutbuster.

"You lost ten accounts today. If everyone in the department lost ten accounts per day, the company would become insolvent in approximately six months."

"How many accounts do the others lose per day?"

"Usually none. One per month at most. Zimbo, you just set the all-time record for the Trifecta Insurance Company, and I'm beginning to lose faith in your people skills. I'll give you one more day to turn things around. If you fail, I'll ask for a replacement. The personnel department can then decide whether to fire you outright or move you to another position more in line with your skills and abilities."

Four days later, Zimbo arrived for work at five o'clock in the afternoon. The personnel department had concluded that his skills and abilities were best suited for the work of a janitor, which would not require him to interact with angry customers. As the employees in the marketing department walked out to the elevators, Zimbo pushed a vacuum cleaner toward the large room from which they were making their escape.

When he was growing up in Chicago, many years before, Zimbo had often vacuumed the living room carpet for his mother. He liked that job. It gave him pleasure to divide the floor into geometric shapes and sweep every one of them without missing an inch. The carpet always looked better when he'd finished, and his mother always praised his work.

So Zimbo didn't mind the work of a janitor. It reminded him of a happy childhood, and the job had one other advantage.

The men and women in the janitorial department belonged to a labor union, unlike the workers in the customer service department. From his first day on the job, Zimbo earned more money per hour than he ever would have earned at his old job had he worked there for fifty years. And as he vacuumed and mopped and dusted, no one would ever call him an idiot, cancel her insurance, or threaten to dynamite the room where all the janitors would gather at nine o'clock that night to enjoy their supper.

◉ ◉ ◉

At one-thirty in the morning, Zimbo and the other janitors took the elevator down to the lobby and went outside, where everybody told everybody else to have a nice weekend. Then they all departed in various directions. Zimbo walked home, climbed the stairs, and put himself to bed.

Four hours later, he awoke from a blissful dream in which he'd watched a skywriting airplane inscribe a company's ticker symbol on an azure sky. Zimbo quickly found a pencil and a piece of paper and wrote down the letters from his dream— BAMI. Then he lay down and went back to sleep.

He awoke at ten o'clock, just as he had every morning since becoming a janitor. After breakfast, he walked to the nearest library and grabbed the first available computer. He typed in the number on his library card, then typed his password—South-SeaBubble—and waited for the machine to reveal its secrets to a tremulous world.

Once Zimbo had entered the website for MoneyWorld. com, the letters BAMI led him to an entry for Baltic Miracle, a company in Wisconsin that bottled and distributed "artesian mineral water guaranteed to restore both men and women to the vigor of youth." Zimbo immediately understood that "the vigor of youth" referred, not to athletics or ballroom dancing, but to one of life's most exquisite pleasures, a pleasure even more exquisite than a visit to Wrigley Field or the Taj Mahal, depending on individual preferences.

A search of online newspaper files quickly revealed to Zimbo that various learned brethren had claimed that Baltic Miracle's restorative artesian mineral water was nothing more than tap water in a fancy bottle. Regardless of these claims, Baltic Miracle's bottled water was still selling like Templeton Rye in 1925.

But at the present moment, Zimbo had no need for artesian miracles. He needed money in large amounts, after which he would enjoy martinis, cigars, and housing that wouldn't put lumps on his head. And once he had that money, perhaps Maria would never leave him. She'd never said she might leave him, but his previous relationships with women had not set records for longevity.

On Monday, at four-fifteen in the afternoon, Zimbo walked into Cobalt Brokers, where he had to wait for ten minutes while Bradstreet talked an elderly woman out of two thousand dollars for a hundred shares of Disco Magic (DIMA). The magic of disco had died sometime in the previous century, but Bradstreet swore on his mother's grave that it was coming back like the dandelions in May.

While he was waiting, Zimbo told Maria how much he loved her. She responded that she liked him, but not much, which meant that she wanted him to flatter her, which he promptly did.

The customer with Bradstreet finally left, muttering something about disco madmen, and Maria directed Zimbo into the presence of the broker.

"Zimbo!" Bradstreet said.

Zimbo cut off Bradstreet's welcome speech. "JB," he said, "how many shares of Baltic Miracle can you get me for a hundred dollars?"

Bradstreet fiddled with his computer. "Five, Zimbo," he said. "I can get you five big ones. That's a nice stock. Good job, Zimbo."

Zimbo tossed the money on Bradstreet's desk.

"Payday must have come early this month," Bradstreet said as he counted the money.

"Not really. I borrowed it from my landlady. I told her my mother was deathly ill."

"Is she really that sick?"

"No. My mother died ten years ago."

"Clever, Zimbo, very clever."

"I can't talk now. Gotta go to work."

"Just one thing, Zimbo."

"What?"

"I need three dollars to execute the trade."

Zimbo fished around in his pocket until he found three dollars in dimes, nickels, and quarters. "There you go," he said. "Make sure you do that as soon as the market opens in the morning. I have a good feeling about this one."

"Consider it done, Zimbo. Consider it done."

"One other thing."

"Yes?"

"What does short selling mean?"

"It's complicated, Zimbo. Don't worry about it."

⊚ ⊚ ⊚

Zimbo arrived for work at four-fifty the next afternoon. "A man called for you," Jill the boss said. "He said it was very important. You can use the phone in my office."

Jill's office was about the size of a telephone booth. People who have the really important jobs always get the smallest offices. Zimbo knew that if Trifecta's CEO left, someone else would grab the job, and nothing about the company would change. But if no one cleaned the toilets, the world would end. He punched in the telephone number. "Hello," said an impossibly friendly voice.

"Julian, I told you not to call me at work. This better be important."

"I think it is, Zimbo. I think it is. Baltic Miracle jumped from twenty dollars a share to over a hundred today. If you can repeat that performance, you're going to become very popular. How did you pick it, Zimbo? What's the secret?"

Zimbo stammered for three or four seconds. "I can't say," he finally blurted. "I'll tell you some other time. Gotta go to work." Later, as he buffed a newly waxed hallway, he saw something blue appear on the floor after he passed over it. He stopped and looked closer. "Do you see that?" he said to one of his work-mates, a woman named Freda.

"Do I see what?" she said.

"The blue letters on the floor. They say GDBK."

"No, I don't see anything like that," she said. "Do you feel okay, Zimbo?"

"I feel fine, Freda. I feel just fine."

◎ ◎ ◎

That night, Zimbo set his alarm for seven-thirty Central Time, an hour before the markets would open in New York. The next morning, five minutes after the alarm woke him and before he made a pot of coffee, he walked down the stairs and knocked on the first door. "George," he said, "may I use your phone?" George looked annoyed. "I'll give you five dollars," Zimbo said, holding up a fiver.

George stopped looking annoyed. Five bucks would easily pay for his minimum daily requirement of Thunderbird from Discount Liquors. "Come right in," he said. "Come right in."

Zimbo handed him the five, grabbed the phone, and dialed. "Zimbo, my friend," Bradstreet said. "What do you have for me so early in the morning? More mystery ticker symbols?"

"Exactly, GDBK. How fast can you get me a margin account?"

"Whoa, Zimbo. Slow down. I'm afraid your investment history doesn't justify a margin account of any size. I'll need cash."

"Maybe my sister would help out if she could profit from this gold mine. What does GDBK stand for?"

"That's GoodBank, Zimbo. Believe it or not, a couple of bright boys decided to clean up the image of their Wall Street bank, and that's how they tried to do it. They thought a new name might create a new image. So far it's a complete failure. It should open this morning at around two dollars. How many shares do you want?"

"A thousand."

"If you can get two thousand dollars, I can get you a thousand shares. Go to it, big guy."

Zimbo quickly made another telephone call. It took him ten minutes to convince Phyllis that he'd seen a vision that would make both him and her as rich as pecan pie. She finally agreed to lend him a thousand dollars, half of what he wanted, but still enough to buy five hundred shares. She decided to use another thousand to buy five hundred shares for herself. Then she picked up Zimbo and drove the two of them to Cobalt Brokers.

They walked inside, where she said, "Zimbo, if you don't pay me back, I'll strangle you."

"I'll pay it back. I promise."

Phyllis conducted her business and walked out, after which Bradstreet made an announcement. "Zimbo, I have so much confidence in these miracle tickers of yours that I'm gonna buy five hundred shares for myself. I'll keep a close eye on this stock all day. Do you want me to sell when it leaves earth orbit?"

"Yes."

"Stop in after three."

"Will do." Zimbo walked back to his apartment, filled the teakettle, and grabbed the coffee.

◎ ◎ ◎

That afternoon, Zimbo stopped at Cobalt Brokers shortly after three o'clock. "Go right in, Zimbo," Maria said. "Don't let him hug you. He'll crack your ribs."

"Zimbo!" Bradstreet shouted as he emerged from his bunker. "You are the man."

"How'd we do?"

"The computers are still catching up, but the close will be about twelve hundred per share. I sold at eleven hundred. I hope that meets with your approval."

"It does." Zimbo's onboard calculator did the arithmetic. "My God," he said. "That's half a million dollars plus change."

"You got it, Zimbo. Maria did all right, too, although she didn't get in until I saw what was really happening and told her about it. She bought a thousand dollars' worth at ten dollars a share."

"I had to borrow the money from my mother," Maria said.

Zimbo looked at Maria until she blushed. "This requires Champagne," he said. "You want to go out for dinner?"

"Aren't you going to work?"

"I think I'll call in sick."

◉ ◉ ◉

Zimbo walked to Cobalt Brokers the next morning to pick up a check for his new fortune. He planned to arrive about seven-thirty, when Bradstreet normally opened for business. But when Zimbo pulled the door, it was still locked. He made a tunnel with his hands, put his face up close, and looked through the glass door. No one was home. He knocked. No one answered. Dark suspicions entered his mind. Bradstreet wasn't there, and neither was Maria. Maria's absence worried him more than Bradstreet's.

"Hey, Zimbo," a woman's voice said.

Zimbo turned around and felt sudden relief. "Maria," he said, "what's happening?"

"I don't know," she said.

Zimbo starred at her as she walked over in her white summer dress, which stopped five inches above her knees. She had the kind of legs that would stop a freight train. She came so close that Zimbo felt the warmth of her body. "I just tried to call him at home," she said, "but no one answered. I hope he's not dead."

Zimbo stopped thinking about Maria's legs. "I hope he's not in Rio," he said.

"My God," she said. "Do you really mean that?"

He reached over and held her hand. "I really do," he said.

⊚ ⊚ ⊚

The Omaha field office of the FBI stands at 4411 South 121st Court on the west side of the city. The building is four stories tall and has the appearance of a long white box with horizontal rows of tinted windows.

One week after the sudden departure of Julian Bradstreet, Zimbo and Maria found themselves sitting with Special Agent Charles Sorenson in an interview room on the second floor of the building. The agent was a tall slender man with gray hair and a face that showed his determination to survive until retirement. "I want to thank both of you for your patience," he said. "This is the boldest operation this fellow has carried out so far, and I needed time to sort everything out."

"We understand," Zimbo said. "We're not in a hurry." Maria nodded in agreement, although both of them actually were in a hurry to recover the money they'd lost and the wages Maria had not collected. Then there was the money that Zimbo owed Phyllis and the money that Maria owed her mother. But Sorenson didn't bring up the unpleasant subject of lost money.

"He used the name Julian Bradley for real estate fraud in Fargo. This is a trick a professional criminal will sometimes use to avoid embarrassment if he runs into two people who know him by different names. He can always just refer to himself as Julian and ignore the surnames."

"Very clever," Maria said. "Rotten but clever."

"How did he set up this Cobalt office in Omaha without getting caught?" Zimbo said.

"He didn't set up a real brokerage. He simply rented a small office, rented some furniture, and slapped up a sign."

"How did he buy the shares of stock?" Zimbo said.

"In most cases, he didn't buy them at all. He just pocketed the money. He kept things going with something resembling a minor Ponzi scheme. When he'd made enough money and things started to get complicated, he simply disappeared."

"How did he pay the ones lucky enough to get their money?" Zimbo said.

"With checks."

"He was very secretive about that," Maria said. "He never wanted me to help him. Now I know why."

"And we now know what bank he used," Sorenson said, "the First National Bank of Northfield, Minnesota. The checks carried the name of an imaginary company he called the Associated Brokers of America."

"This Northfield bank wasn't same one the James and Younger brothers tried to rob, was it?" Zimbo said.

"Yes, it was. He seems to have quite an interest in criminal history. Unfortunately for us, he closed his Northfield account before we figured out all these things. He walked out of the bank with thousands of dollars in cash."

"Now what?" Zimbo said.

Sorenson didn't exactly hang his head in grief, but he did clear his throat a couple of times. Then he said, "We'll keep looking for him, but it's not likely we'll catch him any time soon because he never uses the same scam more than once."

"How does he pass himself off as someone else so easily?"

"Criminals of this caliber have a lifetime supply of social-security cards, driver's licenses, and passports. All he has to do is change his name. We can be sure that he'll never call himself Julian Bradstreet again."

"I assume he made up this GoodBank miracle just for the fun of it."

"Actually," Sorenson said, "that's one thing we don't understand. The GoodBank shares really did make that remarkable run before dropping like a brick the next day. No one knows how or why it happened—not the New York Stock Exchange, not the Securities and Exchange Commission, not anyone. It seems like a miracle, but the FBI deals with facts, not miracles."

Zimbo decided not to pursue the issue of the miraculous ticker symbols. He wanted Agent Sorenson to take him seriously. "What did Bradstreet do with the money we gave him for GoodBank?" he said.

"In that case, he actually bought the shares at Fast Trade Deluxe. And he withdrew the money in three separate checks that he immediately cashed at three local banks where he maintained personal checking accounts. With all that money, he was happy to disappear, leaving all kinds of expensive things in his apartment, including several nice suits. Those may lead us to where he's been, but not where he's going."

"So there's probably no way we can get our money back, is there?" Maria said.

Sorenson paused and looked to one side. "It's not likely," he said, looking back at Maria. "We might get part of it back if we catch him, but that's not likely either. He'll move to some other part of the country, use a new name, and start a different kind of scam when he needs the money. He's an accomplished operator."

After Sorenson thanked them again and said goodbye, Zimbo and Maria left the building and walked to the bus stop, where Zimbo cautiously touched Maria's hand. "Do you still like me a little bit," he said, "despite all the money you lost?"

"I still like you, Zimbo, now more than ever."

"Won't your mother blame me for what you lost?"

"No. She likes you, and you know it. Besides that, you still have your job, and I'll get another one. We can pay everyone back."

"I don't know why you even care about me," he said. "I'm not rich, I'm not good looking, and I'm two inches shorter than you. What do you see in me?"

Maria ran her hand through his hair and kissed him. "It's complicated, Zimbo," she said. "Don't worry about it."

THE
WITNESS

When Robert Dell killed Howard Glover, my father said they shouldn't even have a trial. They should just shake his hand and give him a train ticket back to Kansas.

Our farm bordered Glover's on one side, and my father never could agree with the old man about whose fence was at fault when someone's cattle got out. "He expects me to keep up his fences *and* mine," Dad used to say, scratching angrily at his black moustache.

In addition to his bias against Glover's fences, my father always claimed the old man had cheated him one time. Glover had agreed to buy fifteen Angus steers from Dad, and when it came time to write the check, they had different recollections of the price they'd agreed on. Glover was sure they'd said eighteen cents a pound. My father was sure they'd said twenty. Because of hostilities like these, my dad disliked the old man so much that he told me never to set foot on the Glover place.

My father's reaction to the shooting wasn't unusual. Almost everyone who knew Glover disliked him. The old man was rich enough, but he hadn't made many friends getting that way. In a community that depended on trust, no one trusted Howard Glover.

Against my mother's wishes, my father took me with him to the trial. "It'll give him nightmares," she said, rattling some pans on the stove. She didn't know I was already having nightmares about the whole episode.

"It'll be good for him," Dad said. I don't know what he meant by that, but in any event, he took me with him.

The trial lasted two days, but we went to it only on the second day. I still remember where Dad parked our old Pontiac coupé on the east side of the town square. The forlorn sound of a Hank Williams song drifted through the screen door of a tavern. Next door someone was changing the letters on the marquee of the Iowa Theater. My mother sometimes gave me a dime for a Saturday matinee at the theater. I'd sit there happily while Roy Rogers shot the guns out of the outlaws' hands.

Robert Dell didn't shoot that way.

As far as I could tell, the betting on the courthouse lawn was running heavily in favor of acquittal. My father told a man in overalls that no jury in Fox County would ever convict anyone for shooting Howard Glover. "He did us all a favor," he said, his tan face rigid with certainty. The other man said he agreed.

As we walked toward the courthouse, the heat from the sun reflected off the building's limestone walls. The courthouse had a mansard roof, quoins marching up its numerous corners, and tall narrow windows. High atop the clock tower, a statue of the Roman goddess of justice symbolized truth and fairness.

We climbed the steps and walked into the coolness of the first-floor hallway. On the second floor, someone had already drawn the shades over the windows in the courtroom. The judge's walnut desk shone darkly under the electric lights.

The jury consisted of twelve men in work clothes, men who weren't accustomed to sitting down all day. The judge came in after the jury, and the second day of the trial began.

By the time the opposing sides finished their opening statements, it had grown hot in the courtroom. I couldn't feel the slightest breeze from the old ceiling fans and wondered what good they were.

The first witness for the prosecution was Glover's son, Maxwell, a short broad-faced man about forty. He testified that his father was still alive when he found him and that his last words were "The boy saw it." He swore that his father was unarmed the day he was killed, and Sheriff Adcock later testified that he'd found no weapon on or around Glover's body.

The county attorney then called Maxwell's son Arnie to the stand. Arnie was about the same age I was, and he looked awfully small up there, with his freckles and green eyes, surrounded by all those grownups. He said he'd seen the whole thing from where he was hiding behind the pond bank. "Mr. Dell told Grandpa he promised more for the calves," Arnie said, "but Grandpa said he didn't." Arnie pushed his hair up out of his eyes. He had the kind of hair that never stayed where he wanted it.

"What did Mr. Dell do then?" the county attorney said as he wiped the sweat from his face with a handkerchief.

"He told Grandpa he wasn't going to haul those calves all the way back to Kansas. Then he pointed a gun at him and said he'd better pay what he promised." Arnie looked at his father from time to time as he talked.

"What did your grandpa say to that?"

"He said he might as well put that gun away 'cause he wouldn't pay him another penny."

"Then what happened?" The county attorney shoved his handkerchief into his back pocket and glanced at the jury.

"Mr. Dell called Grandpa a bad name and shot him with his gun." Arnie sat with his hands clasped between his knees.

"Did your grandpa at any time threaten to shoot or hurt Mr. Dell in any way?"

"No."

Arnie's story was convincing enough, except that it sounded as if someone had coached him. That was obviously how it sounded to the defense attorney, and he soon had Arnie caught in a tangle of contradictions.

During the break before the defense began its case, Dad took me downstairs and bought each of us a five-cent bottle of Coca-Cola out of a red vending machine. I drank my Coke and smeared the beads of condensation over the ribbed surface of the bottle while the adults around me talked about the trial. A man with a cigarette told my father he didn't believe a word of Arnie's story.

When the trial resumed, Dell took the stand in his own defense. He confirmed right off what everyone already knew, that he'd shot Howard Glover with a .38-caliber revolver. He also pointed out that he'd immediately turned himself in to the sheriff.

"What led up to the shooting?" said the defense attorney, a trim-looking man from Topeka.

"We got into an argument about the price he'd offered me for the steers," Dell said. He sat back in the chair and spoke confidently. His black hair was neatly combed.

"Did you threaten Mr. Glover in any way?"

"No, I did not."

"Did *he* threaten you?" The lawyer bent forward.

"Yes, he did. He said he'd kill me before he'd pay me another dime." The room was extremely hot by then, but Dell looked cool in his light-gray suit.

"Then what happened?"

"He reached for his back pocket, and I knew he carried a gun there, so I pulled mine and shot first."

"And why did you have a gun with you?" The lawyer pushed his rimless glasses up on his nose.

"Force of habit. I always carry one back home because of the rattlesnakes." He gestured easily with his right hand.

"So is it your testimony that you shot Howard Glover in self-defense?"

"Yes, it is. He said he'd kill me, and I thought he meant it."

In his cross-examination, the county attorney concentrated on the guns. Dell insisted that he had not intended to shoot anyone the day he arrived at Glover's farm. He had his gun along, he repeated, only because of the snakes.

He did have to admit that he never actually saw Glover's gun, but he said everybody knew the old man usually carried one. And several people later testified for the defense that they'd often seen Glover with a pistol stuck in his back pocket.

During his final argument, the county attorney said that since Glover did not have a gun with him the day of the shooting, it was clear that Dell had not acted in self-defense. "The two men quarreled over money," he said to the jury, "and Robert Dell shot Howard Glover out of anger, not fear. Therefore, you have no choice but to find him guilty of murder." He said this without much force. He looked like a man who needed a cold shower.

When his turn came, the defense lawyer argued that Dell had acted reasonably and legally in response to Glover's threats and movements, regardless of whether the old man had a gun with him or not. "Several witnesses have testified that he usually did carry one," he said, "and Mr. Dell had no reason to think otherwise on this occasion, especially after Mr. Glover had threatened to kill him."

Dell's lawyer ended his case by saying it was obvious that Arnie, the state's main witness, hadn't really seen the shooting at all. And, as a matter of fact, Arnie told me a few weeks later that he hadn't even gone near the pond that day.

When the jury brought in a verdict of Not Guilty, almost everyone in the room stood up and cheered. If Glover had a lot of mourners, they weren't around that day. My father smiled at me and patted me on the back. From all this, I concluded that the jury had made the right decision. Dad took me across the street to the Royal Café, and each of us had two pieces of apple pie.

As we walked out of the café a little later, we met Dell and his wife on the sidewalk, and my dad introduced me to them. Dell shook my hand, and his pretty wife stooped down and kissed me on the cheek. I felt awfully embarrassed. They left town that night and never came back.

I know now I should've told someone what I saw. I had a clear vantage point from my hiding place behind the pond bank, and I still remember everything perfectly. Dell and Glover stood about ten feet apart on the other side of the pond—Dell tall and lean, Glover short and heavy, both men full of hate. High scattered clouds sailed east, dragging their shadows across the pond. Redwing blackbirds fluttered about in the cattails. I don't know if Glover really saw me or if that's just something Maxwell made up.

Arnie's account of what happened came surprisingly close to the truth in spite of the fact that he wasn't actually there. Dell's exact words were, "Pay me what we agreed on, or by God I'll shoot you right now."

"Then go ahead and shoot," said Glover, a breeze tousling his thin gray hair, "because I'm not paying you another dime." If he had a gun, he kept it out of sight. He didn't make any threats, and he never reached for his back pocket. When Dell took out his revolver, Glover just stared at him, like a man who'd rather die than lose a dollar.

The revolver made a tremendous noise. I'd never heard anything louder than a .22-caliber rifle before that. Glover fell back on the yellow clay, his arms and legs sprawled out like a puppet's. The redwings flew away through the cottonwoods, Dell walked around the body toward his truck, and I ran like the devil for home.

As I said, I know now that I should've told someone, but I didn't know it then. I wasn't supposed to be there in the first place, and I was afraid I'd get in trouble with my parents. Besides that, from what my father and everyone else said, I wasn't sure Dell had done anything wrong. Adults forget that little kids take them literally. I thought people would get mad at me if I told.

It really doesn't matter anymore. I don't know who I'd tell now or who would care. Maxwell Glover died of a stroke ten years ago, and his wife moved to Arizona. Arnie was killed in Vietnam. Dell may still be alive, but who wants to bother an old man?

My father was right about one thing. No jury in Fox County was ever going to convict anyone for shooting Howard Glover. Dad always said the old man got just what he deserved. They're both dead now, buried in the same graveyard. When we decorate my parents' graves every spring, I sometimes put a flower on Howard Glover's. My wife asked me why one time. I told her I owed him something.

SHEEP

AN ESSAY

My room contained a bed, some chairs, and a plastic bag full of clear liquid. The plastic bag went wherever I went—to the toilet, to a window, anyplace. But I spent most of my time in bed, sometimes looking up at the bag, which released the drops that made their way down a tube and into one of my veins.

While I was sitting in a chair, a woman walked into the room, pushed my robe aside, and used electric shears to shave off most of the hair on my body. She never said a word, and she worked as fast as a contestant at a sheep-shearing convention. She may have been a Basque woman. I wanted to ask her, but

I could tell that she was in a hurry and didn't have time to chat about sheep.

She shaved my left leg, my right leg, and the hair that keeps my penis warm. She shaved my chest, skipped my armpits, and removed the bottom half of my beard, leaving me with a Lincolnesque profile that I later found especially becoming, but which no one else ever mentioned. I fished around for a penny so that I could admire Lincoln's beard, but I had no clothes and therefore no pockets. I looked back at the woman, but she had vanished like a lamb in the woods.

I felt around for the top of my head. When I found it, most of the usual hair still seemed to be intact. I don't remember when this shearing took place. In any event, I somehow got back into bed.

At another forgotten time, a man with a mustache and a white coat told me that I might die on the operating table but that most people did not. A woman with blond hair, delicate features, and a white coat stood beside the man. She looked at me sympathetically, just as you might look at a sheep headed for the slaughterhouse. They said goodbye, and after they left I tried not to think about the condemned sheep.

Claire called me, then Emily, or maybe I called them. "You're going to be okay, right?" Claire said. Emily said exactly the same thing.

"Yes," I said, "I'm going to be okay." They seemed to believe me. I didn't tell them I might die on the operating table.

◉ ◉ ◉

A crew of men entered the room. One of them said his name was Andrew. All the men wore blue uniforms. Or maybe they were green or something else. Janet was there, but I don't remember her colors. The men pushed the bed, with me on it, out the door and down the hallway. I held what I thought was Janet's hand. It was, in any event, someone's hand.

We somehow got into another hallway, where I still held what felt like Janet's hand. Then Andrew said something to Janet, and the hand went away. A set of doors waited at the end of the hall, but before we got there, I went to sleep.

I slept for two days, maybe longer. When I finally woke up, I wondered what day it was. My wristwatch tells the date and the day of the week. I may have had the watch with me, but I couldn't find it. I looked around. There were wires all over the floor, plugged into all kinds of things. I saw the danger in this. Someone could trip and fall down. I went around the room, unplugging all the wires. There were hundreds, thousands. I worked like a Basque shepherd. No one stopped me because no one else was in the room.

Then I found myself back in bed. Beyond the foot of the bed, a tall woman with a long white coat was sorting papers. A bright light glowed beyond her. She had blond hair, but I never saw her face because she never turned in my direction. "It's very dangerous to unplug the wires," she said. "You might cause an accident, or even a fatality!"

"Fatality." What a strange word to use in a roomful of wires. I would have laughed, but I'd forgotten how. I could tell the woman was crazy, but I didn't argue with her. I went back to sleep.

While I was asleep, I had a dream, a vision from God. I'd never had a vision before. It was quite a show. I saw a collection of tablets all around me, similar to the tablets of stone that God gave to Charlton Heston or the tablets of gold that God gave to Joseph Smith, although Smith somehow misplaced his tablets. I don't know what Heston did with his.

The tablets in my vision were different. They were made of typewriter paper with large block letters printed on them. Each piece of paper appeared in a frame made of dark-brown wood. The words on the tablets gave the answers to all the great mysteries that people have been unable to solve throughout all of human history. They answered questions like "If God made the universe, who made God?" I read all the sentences on the tablets, and they all made perfect sense.

I wanted to write down everything I saw on the tablets because I knew I was having a dream and that the tablets would be gone when I woke up, but I didn't have any paper or anything to write with. But the writing on the tablets was so clear and understandable that I knew I'd remember it when I woke up.

But I was wrong. When I woke up, I remembered the tablets but not the words. And it was hard to think about the words because I had a pain in my chest that made me want to start unplugging things. I looked around for the plastic bag, but it had vanished. A nice young woman gave me some pills, but they were as useless as the lost memories of my dream.

I asked Janet to get me some brandy, but I don't think she did. I apparently said all kinds of things to different people, but I don't remember any of it. Steve says I talked about Gabriel García Márquez. Maybe I thought García Márquez could help me remember what was on the tablets in my vision. But he lived somewhere in Mexico, and I lived somewhere in Iowa. I had no way to find him.

I don't remember talking to Steve, but there were a lot of shadows wandering in and out of the room. If he says he was there, I'm sure he was. I stayed in the hospital for eight days. Then Janet drove me to a drugstore, where I learned that I couldn't walk more than a few yards without stopping to rest. I finally got all the drugs I needed. Then Janet drove me home.

All these things happened years ago. I feel better now. I can drive my car and fix my own food. I can climb stairs and type on the computer. But now, after all this time, sometimes the hospital, the tablets in my vision, and even the sheep that covered the green hills where I grew up all seem like forgotten dreams.

WELCOME TO BRANSON

If you want to get ahead in business, you have to pay attention to details. The average tourist in Branson, Missouri, drinks six cans or bottles of Dr Pepper per day, not including holidays, when the average goes up to eight cans or bottles. When I saw the potential, I bought a twelve-ton delivery truck equipped with license plates I'd found in a bus barn one night.

"Son," Dad said when I parked the truck in the front yard, "for a ten-year-old boy, you got a real head for business."

For the soft-drink industry in Branson, I adopted the rapid-response technique of the LAPD for sales and delivery. As soon as the tourists got off the bus, off-duty cheerleaders began selling them an addictive mixture of baking soda, corn sweeteners, tap water, and two ounces of genuine Dr Pepper.

As I grew older, I began branching out. It was just fine to hire local cheerleaders to greet busloads of tourists, but I quickly saw that I was in a slow-growth industry. What if I ran the tours and the buses? The potential was limitless. All I needed was a barn full of sales people and a high-octane boss to keep them on the phone all day. I hired Cousin Willie Portico as soon as he got kicked out of high school. At the age of twelve, I took on the big boys of the industry with my new company—Maxwell Doric (not my real name) Entertainment.

Willie collected an all-male staff of dropouts, coke heads, and reform-school graduates. The girls from Branson refused to work for Willie. He was a good-looking boy with a melodious voice. But by the age of sixteen, he'd already acquired a long list of paternity cases, all of which awaited litigation.

Willie's new employees moved into the haymow of an abandoned barn I'd found on a gravel road just off Route 65 north of town, where an off-duty telephone technician had installed fifty telephones for an address that didn't exist. I kept him on retainer. I'd soon need someone to hook up fifty computers, which I would obtain from John Cornice, a former FBI agent who lived at the bus depot and sold computers out of the attic. You could always count on Cornice for bargain prices.

Seated on hay bales (the small old-fashioned kind) at their respective telephones, the salesmen received a quick training module, with Willie providing examples of how to make a sales call. Using a speaker phone, he punched in numbers from the Omaha telephone book. "Mr. Quoin," he said. "How are you today?"

"Okay, I guess."

"You sound kind of down. Maybe a trip to Branson would make you feel better."

"Where?"

"Branson, Missouri. Greatest collection of entertainment in the world. Bound to perk up your spirits."

"Oh yeah, Branson. I've heard all about it."

"Ever been there?"

"No."

"We're offering some great tours at the lowest prices allowed by law. Would you like to go?"

"No. I don't ever want to go there. Makes me sick to think about it."

"Why's that? Don't you like old people?"

"I am an old person."

"How about a trip to the Smokies?—" The line went dead. Willie looked at the telephone as if it were a timber rattler.

Recovering quickly—which one often needs to do in the telephone sales business—Willie smiled happily and hung up the phone. "Boys," he said, "I just gave you a lesson in how not to sell a tour. Don't get too pushy. Give the customer time to think. Bring him along slowly and patiently. Now, who wants to try the next call?"

Norvel Gable stood up. "I'll do it," he said. Norvel had a slack-jawed appearance and tended to drool on everything he touched. He started walking toward Willie's pulpit, but everyone knew that Norvel had never used a telephone before and couldn't learn anything quickly except how to impregnate close relatives.

"Norvel," Willie said, "I'll help you later. Go back to your hay bale."

I began to wonder if Willie was the right cousin for the job, but he was sixteen and I was only twelve. Family conflict could kill a company when the CEO was my age. All the paperwork I'd filled out said I was forty-eight. Willie's advanced age gave credibility to the haymow.

While Willie trained the staff for assembly-line sales, I went back to work on tour selection, which I knew would make or break the business. Dressed in my Tom Sawyer outfit, I began hanging out at the Branson Tourism Center (BTC), selling soft drinks to the tourists. "Ain't he cute," an old woman said.

"Gimme a bottle of that Dr Pepper, sonny," a man said. "Here, keep the change."

"Gee, thanks, mister," I said. The change amounted to only a nickel and four pennies, but I didn't complain. I intended to collect a large tip from myself before my next birthday.

Because I was so cute and didn't get in the way, the staff at the Branson Tourism Center gave me the run of the place. I overheard all their secrets about upcoming shows months in advance, and I stole customers away from competitors who'd never heard of Maxwell Doric Entertainment. My company led all others in selling package deals for *NOAH the Musical*. I stole my advertising copy straight from the BTC. "Relive an amazing time in history," my ads said. "Experience the enduring faith of Noah and his family."

In only a few days of rapid-response sales, Willie and his team sold tour packages to entire church congregations in Baton Rouge, Birmingham, Tupelo, and hundreds of other towns. Churches that promoted speaking in tongues, faith healing, or snake handling supplied the most buyers. Members of the more-traditional denominations were less inclined to spend over fifty dollars per head to watch stage shows of any sort in the Ozark Mountains, especially one in which Noah danced with a broom.

Despite the objections that some people had about *NOAH the Musical*, the show was one of the best sellers Maxwell Doric Entertainment enjoyed that season. Customers arrived *en masse*, bringing with them all the money they'd saved by not sending their children to school to learn how to read and write, an extravagance they found unnecessary in view of the fact that the world would end in a month or two. Their boys and girls, therefore, would never be able to read the instructions on a box of prophylactics before they began copulating like the monkeys and marsupials on Noah's Ark.

The same year that I introduced *NOAH the Musical* to discriminating audiences from Biloxi to Bakersfield, I left the harbor ahead of all rivals with the "World's First Tribute to the Dogs Onboard the *Titanic*." This compelling tribute could be found at the *Titanic Branson*, which the BTC called the world's largest museum attraction. Potential visitors were assured that two spaniels, Molly and Carter, welcomed guests aboard from nine to five daily. The price of a family pass for two adults and four children was only $62, less if ordered through Maxwell Doric Entertainment.

During their time at the world's largest museum attraction, captivated visitors could, among other activities, enter the *Titanic Branson* through an iceberg, learn how many dogs were on the *Titanic* and how many survived, and listen enraptured to true stories about the dogs that sailed on the *Titanic*. Each child would also receive an educational bookmark, regardless of whether he or she could read a book or anything else.

One could also send Molly and Carter an email message. In my adaptation of this promotional material, I promised that Molly and Carter would send email replies to all messages they received. I also assured the customers that Molly and Carter had no affiliation, religious or otherwise, with Noah or any members of his family, and that Noah would not dance with a broom aboard the *Titanic Branson*.

While hard at work one afternoon, Norvel said, "Willie, I got a little boy on the phone who wonders when he'll get his email from Molly."

"Tell the little fart that Molly went down with the ship."

"He sounds real sad," Norvel said.

"Norvel, you rat-faced hillbilly, hang up and make some calls."

Willie couldn't abide an interruption. "If anyone else gets calls like that," he shouted, "tell the little shits they got the wrong number. Just because we said Molly and Carter would send emails doesn't mean they really will. Molly and Carter are too stupid to chew their food."

Norvel looked kind of unhappy, but he got settled on his bale and started punching phone numbers again.

Altogether, I listed over one hundred shows, attractions, and events for Maxwell Doric Entertainment's first season. Many of these shows, attractions, and events did not exist, but we lost nothing in the transaction because Willie's boys always collected the money in advance, cash being the preferred medium of exchange. We also accepted checks, all of which I immediately cashed at the nearest payday loan shop. Credit cards required too many revealing details about the business and its CEO, so Willie taught the boys to say, "I'm terribly sorry, but we're unable to absorb the fees required for credit cards. But it's absolutely safe to send cash to post office box nineteen twenty-nine, Branson, Missouri."

"Son," my dad said one day, "sometimes I'm afraid you're penitentiary bound."

"Dad," I said, "don't worry. I've got a sure-fire exit strategy."

No matter what package or packages the customers chose, I wanted all of them to take "*The Shepherd of the Hills* Historic Homestead Tour" as one of the last events of their stay in Branson. It was bound to relieve them of any desire to find our barn and burn it down. After they completed the tour, I hoped they'd visit Inspiration Tower, where they could ride one of the glass elevators to the top of the 230-foot tower and take in the 90-mile view. For those guests who might get lost while en route to Inspiration Tower, Willie's salesmen advised them to look for a structure resembling a small-town water tank, minus the obscene slogans painted by local juvenile delinquents.

Finally, after leaving Inspiration Tower, breathless and inspired, the typical visitor would want to attend "*The Shepherd of the Hills* Outdoor Play," where, as the Branson Tourism Center promised, "Harold Bell Wright's epic story of love, loss, power, hardship, and the true meaning of life is immortalized every night on our star-lit stage." The cost of all three attractions for one adult amounted to $57.29, less if purchased through Maxwell Doric Entertainment.

People who like a good book may have read Harold Bell Wright's famous novel, *The Shepherd of the Hills*, which was published by Grosset & Dunlap in 1907. For those who haven't read it, I'll give you a few samples. On the first page, it says,

> "In the hills of life there are two trails. One lies along the higher sunlit fields where those who journey see afar,...and one leads to the lower ground, where those who travel, as they go, look always over their shoulders with eyes of dread,..."

The next paragraph goes on with

> "This, my story, is the story of a man who took the trail that leads to the lower ground, and of a woman, and how she found her way to the higher sunlit fields."

The Shepherd of the Hills also contains much stirring dialog. Early in the book, we find this example:

> "'Law sakes!' cried Sammy, looking at the table. 'You don't use all them dishes, do you dad? You sure must eat a lot.'"

Further along, at an exciting moment, a Mr. Ford says,

> "There's a storm comin' 'fore long, an' we got t' git across th' river 'fore hit strikes."

The book runs on this way for 348 pages, sometimes on the higher ground and sometimes on the lower. I wanted to read it all, but I didn't have time. I was trying to run a business, and right then a state sales-tax hotshot wanted to talk to me about certain "irregularities" in my record keeping, the main irregularity being that I kept no records.

An easy option for the reader who doesn't fancy reading 348 pages would be to return the book to the library and check out the movie instead. Henry Hathaway directed the motion picture version of *The Shepherd of the Hills* in 1941, and John Wayne played the starring role. You can't go wrong with John Wayne. The Internet Movie Database comes straight to the point with its tagline for the movie: "Fury in the wild Ozarks! Hatred unleashed on the 'Trail of the Lonesome Pine'!" I thought about watching this exciting movie myself, but I had work to do.

Our first season at Maxwell Doric Entertainment was the best it could be. It was also our last. It's so hard to please the members of the fickle public, most of whom act like spoiled brats. First, people started griping that they never received the tickets they'd paid for. Then those who'd got their tickets complained that the ticket takers at the shows said the tickets were fakes and that the people had to buy real ones to get into the theater. Others complained that we'd sold them tickets for shows that didn't exist. Then there were complaints about the buses that never arrived and the luxury Branson hotels that no one had built. People complained about all kinds of other things, too, so many things that we had to ignore them.

Finally, someone ratted on us, and thirty federal agents descended on the barn at ten o'clock one morning. Luckily, my mole at the Branson Tourism Center had alerted me a day in advance, and all that the agents found were fifty telephones, fifty computers, and fifty hay bales.

Before we made our escape, I paid off all the boys with cash, all except Norvel Gable, who, according to the same mole at the BTC, wasn't quite as stupid as he looked. Cousin Willie and I debated whether we should drop Norvel down a well shaft, but we finally decided to take off with the cash and leave Norvel unpaid and alone.

After paying off the honest members of the staff, bribing a few more public officials, and splitting the remainder with Willie, I still had two million dollars in cash, all that I needed to go into business with one or more Wall Street banks. That's where the big money is, and getting my hands on that money is my life's ambition. I just turned thirteen, and I've learned the value of elevator shoes and a false mustache. I've started to get interested in girls, so I read a book on prenuptial agreements. I'll be looking for a girl with good telephone skills who can charm the nuts off a clothes tree.

The night before I left town, I met my dad on the twelfth fairway of the Murder Rock Golf and Country Club. "Son," he said, "I wish your mother was still alive to see what success you've had. You remember how much faith she had in you, don't you?"

"Yes, I do. I'll never forget it. I wish you'd go to New York with me, Dad. Willie decided to go along, and we'll need your advice."

"Thanks, Son, but I don't think I could adjust to all the honesty of a big city. You can always call me on that safe number your telephone man set up for us. Call me anytime, and I'll do everything I can for you. I'm sure you remember Charley Cornice, my old friend who used to work for the FBI. He promised to check with his contacts now and then and let me know if the feds get wise to you. You can always count on the FBI."

"Thanks, Dad. I'll remember that."

"Goodbye, Son. You'd better get going before the golf carts start rolling this way. Be careful. Never trust a politician or a preacher, and always do the right thing."

"I will, Dad, and as soon as I start to clean up on credit-default swaps, I'll send you a hundred thousand dollars every week or two."

Dad put his hand on my shoulder and looked at me proudly. "You're quite a boy, Son," he said. "You're quite a boy."

RETURN

TO

PHILIPPI

Mark looks through his screen door at the woman who lives on the other side of Macedonia Street. She's wrestling with her mailbox, and she should have an advantage. She's bigger than the mailbox, she has certain cognitive skills, and the mailbox has no skills. The mailbox just hangs there beside the door, under the protective umbrella of the porch.

The postman had no trouble putting the package into the mailbox that morning, but the woman can't get it out. She moved it in a way that wedged it into the space between the box itself and the lid that opens and closes over it. The mailbox is made of one-inch lumber and can't be bent without breaking it. The woman could smash or saw the wood, but Mark understands that she wouldn't want to do that. She knows that she'd have to replace a damaged mailbox, and the new one might be just as much trouble as the old one.

The next day, the postman takes the package out of the mailbox, looks at it, and puts in back in. Later, the woman still can't get it out.

◉ ◉ ◉

"Dr. Octavio," Mark said, "I had a terrible dream."

"I'll be right with you, Mark," Dr. Octavio said. He was looking for something on a shelf behind his desk. He was tall and slim, with black hair and a short black beard. He found a pencil, sat down, and made a note just to see if the pencil was sharp enough. It wasn't.

Mark had often wished that he looked like Dr. Octavio, but he didn't. He was short and bald, with a brown hedge around the bald spot.

"Tell me about your dream," Dr. Octavio said. He had no interest in dreams. He was interested only in symptoms. But he always humored Mark when he talked about his dreams.

"I dreamed that I was married to the woman who lives across the street, and she wouldn't let me get a divorce."

"Describe her for me."

"She has blonde hair that erupts from her head with no pattern or form. It doesn't appear that anyone ever tried to comb it."

"I see."

"She's about six-two and weighs over four hundred pounds. In a rational universe, she'd be playing right tackle for the Green Bay Packers."

"You said this woman wouldn't let you get a divorce. But given present laws, you wouldn't have to get her permission to get a divorce. How could she stop you in the world of your dream?"

"She'd knock me down and sit on me."

"I see." Dr. Octavio tried again to make a note, but the pencil was still too dull. "Have you ever been married to a woman like this in real life?"

"No, only in this dream."

"Has anyone in real life ever tried to knock you down and sit on you?"

"Yes."

"Who?"

"The woman who lives at the end of the block."

"Why?"

"One night when I was drunk, I peed on her flower bed. It was about midnight, and I figured everyone would be asleep."

"I see. This is the sort of thing people do when they're still teenagers. How old were you?"

"Forty-two."

Dr. Octavio threw the pencil into the wastepaper basket. "Describe this woman for me, Mark."

"She looks exactly like the woman who lives across the street. They're twin sisters. In a rational universe, she'd be playing left tackle for the Green Bay Packers."

⊛ ⊛ ⊛

The next afternoon, right after lunch, Mark stationed himself at the reference desk at the Philippi Public Library. To one side, patrons sat before rows of library computers, staring at countless websites—some of rare value and most of no value. One man, as always, played solitaire until required to surrender the machine to the next person in line. Mark spent most of his time answering questions about how to use the computers. He was always ready to help anyone find useful information about history, literature, or other subjects, but questions about those topics seldom came up.

On the other side of Mark's desk, people sat at a long row of tables and typed earnestly at their laptop computers. These included one man who never missed a day, a man remembered for his bushy gray beard and his consumption of turkey sandwiches. The man himself seemed most attentive to his inability to make his fingers hit the right keys, which led him to a series of muted but profane mutterings.

Beyond the many computers, stacks of shelved books went largely unnoticed.

At two o'clock in the afternoon, a woman entered the room with her sixteen children. The youngest child was eighteen months old. "I want all of you to leave me alone," the woman said. "Go over to the bookshelves and play a game or something."

The woman's progeny withdrew to the fiction section and began a game of hide and seek. The oldest child, a sixteen-year-old girl, took charge. "You're it, rodent," she said to her brother Robert.

"Why me, Cressida? Why not you?"

"Shut up, rodent, or I'll explain with this." She picked up all three volumes of *War and Peace* and prepared to launch an artillery barrage.

Robert withdrew from the battlefield and began the game, which included running, shouting, pushing, and hitting. The eighteen-month-old boy had no interest in this sport. He displayed curly black hair, a summer tan, and a bulging baby tummy full of baby organs. He wore nothing but a pair of diapers.

He wandered down one of the aisles between the book stacks, where he began taking books from the shelves and throwing them over his shoulders. He could reach only the two bottom shelves, but that didn't slow him down. A time-motion study would have found that the boy was working as efficiently as possible for a child of his age and height. At the rate he was going, he could have tossed all the fiction he could reach in about three hours.

After ordering her kids to leave her alone, the woman pulled the chair away from one of the library's computers. The man sitting in the chair was asleep, which prevented any immediate shouting and hitting.

Mark stood up and walked over to the woman, who'd grabbed an empty chair. "Mrs. Burton," he said, "we've discussed this before. You have to wait your turn. I also have to remind you that this isn't a playground or a childcare center. If I have to call the head librarian again, I can't predict what she'll say or do."

"Shut up, guest librarian. Go play with yourself." She sat down on the chair and summoned her favorite website from the computer.

Mark walked back to the desk, picked up the phone, and called Ms. Troy. Five minutes later, one man and one woman in police uniforms followed Ms. Troy to the scene of the crime. They weren't actually twirling their nightsticks, but their business hands were checking various police aids attached to their belts.

"Mrs. Burton," Ms. Troy said. "You've already violated several of the library's rules, and you've only been here for ten minutes. The pornographic website you're looking at is reason enough on its own to ban you from the building."

"Shut up, old fool."

Ms. Troy ignored this insult. Her long experience, neat gray hair, and tasteful blue suit lent authority to her next statement.

"I want you to get up from the computer, gather your children, and leave this library at once," she said.

"And what if I don't?"

"I'll have no choice but to call on the two police officers you see with me." By this point, the policeman and the policewoman had readied themselves for whatever the situation might require. They stood with their arms at their sides, looking at Mrs. Burton. They'd met her before.

Mrs. Burton was small, mean, and as quick as a bobcat. Like a bobcat, she could tear you apart if you cornered her. She looked at the police for two seconds. "Screw 'em," she said.

The librarian stepped out of the way, the people at the computers stared at Mrs. Burton, and the children interrupted their game. Unmoved by all this drama, the eighteen-month-old boy continued his epic removal of the books from the shelves.

The Battle of Philippi was about to begin.

⊙ ⊙ ⊙

"Dr. Octavio," Mark said, "I had a terrible dream."

"Tell me about it, Mark," Dr. Octavio said. He picked up a pencil and began sharpening it with his pocket knife.

"I was a soldier," Mark said, "and a battle was about to begin. Across the valley, a huge army was getting ready to attack."

"Whose army were you in?"

"I don't know. No one ever said. The soldiers had swords and shields, and some of them rode horses."

"Where was this?"

"In the Philippi City Park."

"Go on, Mark."

"Suddenly I noticed that I was the only one in my army. I looked across the valley and saw that all the soldiers on the other side looked exactly like Mrs. Burton."

Dr. Octavio didn't have to ask who Mrs. Burton was. He'd read the article in the *Philippi Bugle*. She was still in jail, and her children were still in the care of the department of social services, where all but the youngest were stealing everything they could move. Showing more respect for public property, the little one was merely throwing everything on the floor. "I understand," the doctor said.

"Well," Mark said, "there was no one else on my side and no one to stop me. So I decided I'd better run away before all the Mrs. Burtons stabbed me with their swords and ran over me with their horses. But when I tried to run, I couldn't move. I thought about calling the police, but all of them were guarding the real Mrs. Burton at the county jail."

"I'm sure you know that the inability to run is common in dreams of this sort," Dr. Octavio said. He finished sharpening the pencil and used it to make a note.

"Yes."

"Are there any people in real life that make you want to run away?"

"Yes, Mrs. Burton. She lives across the street at the end of the block."

"I see," Dr. Octavio said. "Why do you want to run away from her?"

"One of her children stole my mailbox. When I told her about it, she said that I was a liar and that if I ever said anything like that again she'd tear me apart."

"Then what did you do?"

"I bought another mailbox."

⊚ ⊚ ⊚

Mark looked out the window at his new neighbor. The man had moved in the previous day. He had an extremely loud voice and shouted everything he said, apparently unable to lower the volume. When he talked to the cat, he shouted. When he answered the phone, he shouted. Mark could hear everything he said, and the man never said anything he wanted to hear.

The man's face was perfectly square, like a cartoon character's face. He wasn't necessarily ugly, but his shouting combined with his face to make him loathsome. He was the worst neighbor on the block, worse than Mrs. Burton and the two 400-pound sisters.

Mark had gone to the window because he heard the man shouting a greeting to the postman, who was standing about three feet away. When the man shouted, the postman moved farther away. At one point he put his hands over his ears. "My name's Cassius," the square-faced man shouted. "Sure is a nice day."

"Very nice," the postman said, speaking so quietly that Mark could barely hear him. The louder the new neighbor shouted, the more quietly the postman responded. Finally, he shoved the mail into the man's hands and turned to go. "Have a nice day," he whispered.

"You too," the neighbor bellowed. He went back into his house and slammed the door so loudly that it sounded like artillery fire. Mark started his old record player, turned up the volume, and played the 1812 Overture, complete with cannon fire and church bells. Despite these attempts at self-defense, Mark could still hear his neighbor laughing at something on television. Everything that came out of the man's mouth woke everyone within shouting distance.

After a few minutes of this, the large blonde-haired woman across the street ran over and demolished the man's door as she went through it. "What the hell you shouting about?" she screamed.

"What's that?" the man yelled. "Come on over here."

The woman did as requested, and Second Battle of Philippi began. Thirty minutes later, the police cars and the ambulance had come and gone. Mark stepped outside and listened. Only one sound broke the silence. At the end of the block, Mrs. Burton's youngest child pushed the refrigerator over.

◎ ◎ ◎

"Dr. Octavio."

"Yes, Mark." Dr. Octavio counted his pencils as he talked.

"I had a terrible dream."

"Tell me about it."

"In my dream, two people were always shouting about something."

"Who were they?"

"Cassius and the woman across the street. In my dream, they had a terrible fight."

"And what happened in real life?"

"They had a terrible fight. But when Cassius came home from the hospital, they fell in love. Their love is the real nightmare. All day long and most of the night, they shout to each other across the street."

"What do they say?"

"They say how much they love each other. I'd like to hire a hit man and have them liquidated."

The doctor stopped counting and looked at Mark. "Do you know a hit man?" he said.

"No. I didn't meet any in library school."

⊙ ⊙ ⊙

On the first day of the next month, Mark's mortgage payment came due, just as it always did. But this time, he ignored the payment and abandoned the house. He left all his furniture behind and took only his clothes, his toothbrush, his eyeglasses, a blanket, a pillow, and an alarm clock. At two-thirty in the morning, he arrived at the library by cab and let himself in with his staff key.

He found a cardboard box, wrote his name on it, and stored his possessions in a broom closet. Then, after setting the alarm clock, he went to bed in one of the study rooms. The next morning, he told Ms. Troy that he wanted to work all day every day of the week, with occasional time off to run errands. He would do this, he said, without asking for a larger salary.

"You can work all day if you want to, Mark," Ms. Troy said, "but don't you need more time for your social life?"

"No," Mark said, "I've had all the social life I'll ever need." That night, while the janitor went here and there with his mops, brooms, and vacuum cleaner, Mark sent email messages to all his friends and relatives, telling them that his new address was Box 42 at the Philippi Post Office.

As Mark had anticipated, his new life sheltered him from the all the evils of Macedonia Street. Mrs. Burton was banned from the library for life. The twin sisters and the man next door were semiliterate, had no interest in books or computers, and never went to the library. Mark would never hear their voices again.

The next day, Mark walked three blocks to the Philippi Recreation Center, where he walked on a treadmill for thirty minutes, after which he took a shower. His old neighbors never exercised and never took showers. He'd never see them at the recreation center. Every day he found new ways to avoid the residents of Macedonia Street.

"Dr. Octavio."

"Yes, Mark." The doctor plugged in his new pencil sharpener, inserted a fresh pencil, and listened. The machine sounded fine.

"I haven't had any memorable dreams lately."

"Why's that?" Dr. Octavio withdrew the pencil and blew off the shavings.

"I ran away from Macedonia Street and found a new place to live. It's probably against the law. You won't tell anyone, will you?"

"That depends on the law." He made a note with his sharp new pencil.

"I'm living in the library."

"Have you ever read 'Bartleby, the Scrivener'?" Dr. Octavio said.

"That's where I got the idea," Mark said.

"I won't tell anyone."

◉ ◉ ◉

Twenty years later, Mark woke up at nine o'clock on a hot Wednesday morning, got dressed, and folded his blanket. He walked into the employee lunchroom, where he made himself a cup of coffee and a bowl of oatmeal. By the time the library opened at ten, he had taken his position at the reference desk, where he awaited the arrival of the computer people.

One hour later, a young man entered the library and walked over to the fiction section. It always pleased Mark when someone showed an interest in printed books. Most library patrons seemed to think that books were artifacts from the pre-digital dark ages.

The young man was neither tall nor short, carried himself with a confidant air, and had a nice head of dark hair. He stood there awhile, surveying the books. Finally, he reached up, took a copy of *Moby Dick* off the shelf, and threw it over his shoulder.

Mark reached for the telephone. After two decades of peace, the Third Battle of Philippi was about to begin.

DAVID'S
TOE

The man with dark eyes came through the door late one afternoon in July. "I have something I must show you," he said, "in private if I may." He spoke with a foreign accent, perhaps Mediterranean.

Altman locked the front door and closed the shades. He'd done business with other people who felt a need for secrecy, and he'd learned to humor them. Shelley had taught him the value of tact. "Well then," he said, turning back toward the man, "what can I do for you today?"

The man reached into his jacket pocket and pulled out a leather pouch. He opened the pouch, took out a small object, and set it on a display case.

Altman stared at the object. It was a human toe, not a real toe, but one made of stone, apparently marble. "What is it?" he said. "I mean, I can see what it is, but what is it exactly?"

The man gazed at him with his dark eyes. "It is the only thing left from *The Spirit of Brooklyn*," he said. "The rest is dust and gravel."

"Are you sure of this? The authorities say they have no evidence the statue was damaged."

"The authorities seldom have evidence of anything, but I know the men who took the statue. One of them is my brother. They said they would destroy it, but no one believed them."

Altman remembered the threats the thieves had sent to the newspapers, how they would blow the statue to bits if the ransom wasn't paid. But the Brooklyn Advancement Society and the city of New York had held firm. To pay the ransom would encourage similar incidents all over the world, they said.

"All right," Altman said. "Assuming that you're telling the truth, why did you bring this to me? I can't sell it, unless I want to end up in jail."

"I do not want you to sell it, Mr. Altman. I want you to give it back to the Brooklyn Advancement Society and the people of Brooklyn." The Brooklyn Advancement Society had originally commissioned the statue, then later erected it at a park in Brooklyn Heights as a gift to the people of the borough.

"Why not give it back to them yourself? What do you need me for?"

"I cannot give it back in person, Mr. Altman. They might hold me for the police, and then my brother would be implicated. I am taking a chance as it is. I could have thrown it away, but it is far too important for that. I would have felt extremely guilty."

"I don't know. This all sounds pretty unlikely. How do I know this is the real thing?"

"Look at photographs, or replicas. You are an art dealer, Mr. Altman. You know how to detect forgeries."

Altman didn't really think he could detect forgeries, but he was flattered by the suggestion that he could. "Yes, but I'd still need more proof," he said, "before I could make a claim like this. I'd look like a fool if it turned out to be a fake, and fools don't do very well in the art business." Altman wasn't doing very well as it was, but he saw no need to point that out.

"The proof," the man said, "is that I am here at all. I did not have to come here. I do not expect anything in return. I just want to return this to its rightful owners."

The man said all this with such sincerity that Altman started to believe him. He said he'd do what he could and showed the man out.

After closing the gallery that evening, Altman set the marble toe on a counter and stood there looking at it. What would be the best way of delivering it? And what was its value anyway? The man with dark eyes thought it was an important remnant, but was it? Could the statue be reconstructed from this fragment like an ancient mastodon recreated from a few bones? Altman wished he could ask Shelley these questions. He had no one to talk to now that she had left.

He turned on the burglar alarm, locked up, and drove home. He would have to proceed carefully with this statue business. It was a delicate matter, one that could either help him or get him into trouble.

◉ ◉ ◉

The next morning, he called the office of the Brooklyn Advancement Society. The young man who took the call listened politely to his story. Altman told him about the mysterious visitor and the marble toe, then stated his reservations about the matter. He was, he concluded, only trying to help.

The young man said the whole episode sounded like a hoax, but that it would be wise to follow up on it just in case. He said he'd look into the matter. An hour later he called back to say that Mr. Palmer would like to see Altman that afternoon.

Feeling a little apprehensive, Altman arrived at the address in Brooklyn Heights twenty minutes early. He was forty-two years old, but in the presence of authority he still felt like a child. He straightened his tie and knocked on the door of the brownstone mansion.

An elderly female housekeeper ushered him in and left him alone in a dim, silent parlor. After his eyes adjusted to the darkness, he surveyed the objects around him: books with dark bindings in dark bookcases, dark oil paintings on the walls, furniture made of dark wood. Even the lamp in the corner seemed to emit dark light.

Sitting in the darkness, he considered the possibility that *The Spirit of Brooklyn* didn't really deserve all the attention it was getting. In Altman's opinion, David Casteel was hardly an inspiring model for a statue. He'd made a career of portraying naval heroes in tiresome combat movies, movies that were always at their best when he was off camera.

Defenders of the statue saw in Casteel a reminder of Brooklyn's long association with the sea. The statue's critics viewed it as nothing more than a poor imitation of Michelangelo's *David*. Matthew Salazar, the sculptor, had even implied that the statue was a joke. But the public loved it, and that was what made it so valuable.

Mr. Palmer finally swept into the room, and with him came the light. He opened the shades and turned on every light bulb in the room. Still blinking, Altman stood up to shake hands.

Palmer was overweight and partially bald. He had small blue eyes, with which he examined Altman suspiciously. The two men sat down, and Palmer spoke first. "What was it you wanted to see me about?" he said. "Something having to do with the missing statue, wasn't it?" His accent suggested Britain rather than Brooklyn.

"Yes it was," Altman said. "A man brought me what he claimed was part of the statue. I'm at art dealer, you see, and for some reason he thought I should be the one to return it. Not that I actually believed his story, of course. I just wanted to do the right thing."

"What part?"

"I beg your pardon."

"You said this man brought you part of the statue. What part was it?"

"A toe."

"Which toe?"

"The large one."

"Which foot?"

"The right one, I believe." Altman was surprised by the specificity of Palmer's questions.

"Do you have it with you?"

"Pardon?"

"Do you have the toe from the statue with you?"

Altman found Palmer's manner too abrupt. "Yes I do," he said.

"May I see it, please?"

"Certainly." Altman took the toe out of his jacket pocket and handed it over.

Palmer examined it carefully. "This looks like the real thing," he said.

"The man said the thieves had destroyed everything but the toe," Altman said. "He seemed to think that a toe was better than nothing."

Palmer looked up from the toe and gazed at Altman. "Who was this man?" he said.

"I don't know. He didn't give me his name. He said one of the thieves was his brother."

Palmer continued to stare at him. "Mr. Altman," he finally said, "the men who took the statue left word that when they were ready to state their demands, they would produce the large toe from the statue's right foot. This, they said, would establish the validity of the communication." He slipped the toe into his jacket pocket while Altman considered this information. "So you can understand my interest in the particulars of this matter."

"Yes."

"What else did this mysterious man tell you? Did he say anything about a ransom payment?"

"No, he said there was nothing left but dust and gravel."

"Another deception," Palmer said. "They no doubt wanted to make you a better courier by withholding part of the truth. They knew you wouldn't agree to help them if they told you their real plans. I suspect they'll get back in touch with you. Forgive my indirect manner. I made some inquiries about your honesty this morning, and everyone vouched for you. But I still felt the need to be cautious. I'm sure you'll understand."

"Certainly."

"And I hope you'll contact me again as soon as you receive another communication."

"Of course."

"And please tell no one else about this matter. Publicity could destroy our chances of ever recovering the statue."

"I understand."

Palmer showed him to the door.

⊙ ⊙ ⊙

The next morning, Altman opened the gallery at ten o'clock, the usual time. And, as usual, no one was waiting to get in. A real-estate agent, a business consultant, and an article in a trade journal had convinced Altman that the "art scene" would soon be moving from Soho to this section of Flatbush. The art scene had moved nowhere near Flatbush and showed no signs of doing so, leaving Altman saddled with a three-year lease.

The shop was long and narrow and, except for the front windows, lacked any source of natural light. Altman had countered the gloom the best he could by installing an expensive lighting system and painting the walls and ceiling a creamy shade of white. All he needed now was a stream of wealthy customers.

Unfortunately, he wasn't likely to receive a stream of customers, wealthy or otherwise. His gallery was so isolated that well-known artists refused to show there. The artists who did bring him their work were like the gallery itself, unknown and unsought.

In the absence of customers, Altman tried to keep busy around the shop. On this particular morning, he was dusting a sculpture for the second time when the phone rang. "Mr.

Altman," said a familiar voice, "I visited your gallery just two days ago, concerning a fragment from a statue. Perhaps you will recall me."

"Yes, I recall," Altman said.

"I wondered if you had contacted the Brooklyn Advancement Society. You can understand my concern."

"Yes, of course. I spoke to Mr. Palmer yesterday."

"May I ask what his reaction was?"

Altman noticed the man's accent again. It was Lebanese or something similar. He wasn't sure what. "He was very interested," he said, "and suspicious."

"Was he surprised?"

"He didn't appear to be."

"Did you give him the fragment?"

"Yes, I did."

"Excellent. Did you discuss the condition of the rest of the statue?"

"Yes, but he didn't believe the rest of the statue had been destroyed, even though you told me it had."

"Yes, I must apologize for misleading you. Mr. Palmer is quite right. The rest of the statue is intact. It was necessary to tell you otherwise in order to make contact with the society. I am sure you understand."

"Yes." Altman understood, but he didn't like it.

"Mr. Altman, you have been so helpful. I feel I must do something to repay you."

"Oh?" Altman looked around the deserted shop at all the unsold paintings and sculptures. "That really isn't necessary," he said. "I merely wanted to help."

"Mr. Altman, I insist. You have done so much that I must show my gratitude."

Altman looked at the cash drawer. "You really don't need to," he said.

"But I must. Goodbye, Mr. Altman."

⊚ ⊚ ⊚

The next morning, fifteen minutes after Altman had opened the gallery, a woman in a light-blue summer dress came in and asked to see anything Altman had by Maurice October.

"An excellent young painter," Altman said, leading the woman to a painting on the back wall. No one had ever paid any attention to it before, and he had considered taking it down. "A sound investment for someone prepared to keep the piece for an extended period."

The woman glanced at the painting. She had on white gloves and a broad-brimmed hat. "Do you have anything else of his?" she asked.

"I believe so," Altman said. "Let me check." He rummaged around in the back room and came back with seven more paintings by the newly popular Maurice October. "Here we are," he said.

The woman barely looked at the paintings. "How much are they?" she said.

"Five hundred dollars each."

"And the one on the wall?"

"One thousand." He held his breath.

"I'll take them all." She reached into her leather handbag, and Altman exhaled. She pulled out a wad of money and counted out forty-five hundred dollars.

Altman wrapped the paintings and carried them out to the woman's cab. He said thank you several times and waved as the cab pulled away. It didn't bother him a bit that the woman didn't wave back.

His pulse had just returned to normal when a tall blond-haired man walked into the shop. The man had on a white suit and dark glasses. He wanted to see anything Altman might have by Rita Cordoba.

Altman dug six paintings out of the back room, carried them into the showroom, and leaned them against a wall. He thought it strange that the man didn't remove his sunglasses to look at the paintings, but he wasn't about to mention it.

"How much are they?" the man said.

Altman's tongue momentarily refused to say the numbers. "Two thousand each," he finally blurted.

"Wrap them up, please."

Altman didn't have to be convinced. He got busy, pausing only to say how quickly Ms. Cordoba's work was rising in value. The blond-haired man didn't seem interested, and in fifteen minutes Altman shoved another twelve thousand dollars into the cash drawer.

He stayed close to the door the rest of the day in hopes that more art lovers would drop in, but none did. Even so, it hadn't been a bad day. After closing up for the night, he took the money to the bank, went out to dinner, and spent the rest of the evening thinking about what he could do with his share of sixteen thousand five hundred dollars.

At eleven o'clock the next morning, the telephone interrupted Altman's progress with the dust cloth. After picking up the phone and saying, "Altman Gallery," he recognized the voice of the man with dark eyes.

"I hope you are feeling well this morning," the man said.

"I'm feeling fine, thank you," Altman said.

"And I hope your business is prospering."

"It is. Very much so."

"You were so helpful to me the other day that I wanted to request your assistance again."

"I see." Altman hesitated. "What would you like me to do this time?"

"A man will come to your gallery this morning to obtain something you have in your possession. His name is Carpino. He is a representative of the Brooklyn Advancement Society. His coming and going must take place as discreetly as possible. I trust that you will be able to assist him."

"Certainly, but I can't imagine what I might have that he would want. Is it a painting? Or something else? I'm afraid I don't understand."

"Mr. Altman, I hope you will believe me when I tell you that you will be able to give Mr. Carpino precisely what he wants. Please forgive me, but I am not at liberty to tell you what it is. May I depend on you, Mr. Altman?"

"Yes,…I guess so."

"Thank you, Mr. Altman. I hope I will be able to return your kindness."

Altman hung up and began adjusting the overhead lights. He usually felt bored at the gallery, but today he was apprehensive. He felt himself being caught up in events that he couldn't control. The money was nice, but what might it lead to?

At ten minutes after eleven, a man with a black mustache walked into the shop. "Mr. Altman," he said, "my name is Carpino." He spoke with an accent that might have been Italian. Altman couldn't tell. "I am here on behalf of the Brooklyn Advancement Society. I believe you have been informed of my mission."

"Yes," Altman said, "but I have no idea what it is that I'm supposed to give you."

"I believe we will find it in your storage room. If you would lock the front door and close the shades, we could look and see."

"Very well," Altman said. He closed the gallery and walked to the back of the room, where he opened the door, led Carpino into the darkness, and turned on the light. "Now what—" he said as he turned around, cutting himself off in mid-sentence. There in the middle of the room stood *The Spirit of Brooklyn*.

"You see, Mr. Altman, you do have something to give me."

Altman closed his mouth. "I guess so," he said. The object in front of him was clearly the work of Matthew Salazar.

"I am sure you understand the need for secrecy. We have paid a great deal of money to recover the statue. We could not afford to have something go wrong."

"Of course not."

"If you will be kind enough to open the door, we will remove the statue."

Altman unlocked and opened the freight door. A moving van, a forklift, and two large men stood in the brick alley. One of the men drove the forklift into the room, picked up the statue, backed out, and put it into the truck. The other man closed and locked the truck door. The whole operation took less than three minutes.

"Goodbye, Mr. Altman," Carpino said. "On behalf of the Brooklyn Advancement Society and the people of Brooklyn, I extend my warmest thanks." Without another word, he climbed into the cab of the truck with the other two men, and they drove away, leaving the forklift in the middle of the alley.

Altman stood there for a minute. Then he locked the freight door, walked back into the display room, and reopened the gallery. He was glad, for once, that no one came in. He needed time to think. How, he asked himself, had anyone gotten through his elaborate security system?

He'd had the system installed before opening the gallery for business a year before, back when he still believed that he'd be showing valuable works of art. According to the salesman who sold it to him, the security system was impregnable. It employed steel doors, dead bolts, video cameras, an expandable grating for the front of the store, and electronic alarms that connected with Samson Safety Systems, a private security firm. It seemed unbreachable, but someone had breached it, and Altman didn't know how. Once more, he found himself in need of Shelley. She'd be able to figure it out, if she were still there.

While he was pondering this mystery, a middle-aged man rushed into the shop. He was clean-shaven and spoke with a Brooklyn accent. "Mr. Altman," he said, "my name's Carpino. I think you were told to expect me."

The effect this statement had on Altman could not have been more forceful. He staggered backward and almost fell down. "Wh-what?" he stammered.

"You have something for me, don't you? My name is Carpino. I work for the Brooklyn Advancement Society."

"Yes…. I mean no," Altman said. "What do you want?"

"The statue in the back room. You have it, don't you?"

"Yes. I mean I did. You were already here."

"What does that mean?" The man looked quickly around the room.

"Someone called Carpino was here fifteen or twenty minutes ago. He took the statue."

"You mean you *let* him take it? Couldn't you see he was one of them?"

"One of whom?"

"The people who stole the statue. Who else?"

Altman began to see the danger he was in. "Well, how was I to know? He said he was Carpino. For that matter, how do I know that you are and he wasn't?"

The man stared at him for a moment. Then his shoulders sagged and his jaw muscles relaxed. He reached into his jacket pocket, pulled something out, and opened his hand for Altman to see. There on his palm, perfectly illuminated by the gallery's expensive lighting system, lay David's toe.

❋ ❋ ❋

The telephone rang in Altman's apartment at nine o'clock that night. "Mr. Altman, once again I must apologize for misleading you."

"Well," Altman said, "I found myself in a very difficult situation."

"And I am extremely sorry. I did not want to alarm you by saying that two Carpinos would visit you. The real one got there last, you see."

"Yes, I see."

"The first man was actually a colleague from Norway. He does excellent impersonations."

"How fortunate for him."

"This slight deception became necessary when Mr. Palmer announced, at the last moment, that he would not make the second payment until twenty minutes after we revealed the location of the statue. This was a change in plans that we could not tolerate. We became suspicious, Mr. Altman."

"No doubt."

"We sensed the presence of the police."

"I'm not surprised."

"The statue was already in your storage room by then. So we had to take possession of it once more. Your assistance was extremely kind, Mr. Altman, a kindness we will not forget."

"I'm sure you won't, but it puts me in a bad position. Now they suspect me, and I had nothing to do with it. The police were at my shop for almost an hour."

"It is in the nature of the police to be suspicious, Mr. Altman. They lack the quality of trust. But their interest in you will pass, and soon they will forget all about you."

"I hope so. It was no fun, I can tell you."

"For which I again apologize. Goodnight, Mr. Altman."

"Goodnight."

The next morning, the gallery returned to normal. No one but the postman came through the door all day long. Altman did notice something unusual out front, though. A big man in a gray suit sat in a car a little way down the street for the entire day. In fact, the same man sat in the same car for three days.

He divided his time between watching the shop and reading newspapers, showing little enthusiasm for either task.

Finally, both the man and the car disappeared. The following day, a new string of new customers filed through the gallery, buying everything Altman had by Paul Angora, Carol de Metier, and Marcus Lavelle.

Altman was standing beside the cash drawer the next morning when the man with dark eyes walked through the door. "Good morning, Mr. Altman," he said. "I hope you are prospering."

"Thanks, I am," Altman said.

"Perhaps you will not think unkindly of me if I trouble you for another favor."

"Might as well. Just keep the police out of it this time, if you don't mind."

The task was not difficult. Altman was to deliver another message to Mr. Palmer at the Brooklyn Advancement Society. "And please," the man said, "you must be sure to deliver the message at exactly eleven o'clock this morning." Altman looked at his watch. It was already ten-fifteen.

He closed the shop, got into his battered Chevy, drove to Brooklyn Heights, and parked beside a fire hydrant. The Brooklyn Advancement Society's massive house stood a few doors away. Volvos and BMWs lined the street.

At three minutes before eleven, Altman got out of his car, locked the door, and walked down the street. At precisely eleven o'clock, he pushed the button for the doorbell.

Palmer himself opened the door this time. The housekeeper was nowhere in sight. Palmer wasted no time. "Where is it?" he said.

"On Staten Island," Altman said, "in a moving van in the parking lot at Snug Harbor."

"Are you sure?"

"That's what he told me."

Palmer closed the door without another word. Altman felt disappointed. He would've liked another look inside the big house, but he knew why Palmer was in a hurry. He went down the steps, walked back to his car, and started the engine.

Now that he had completed his errand, Altman decided to go to Greenwich Village for lunch. He drove across the Brooklyn Bridge and found an expensive parking lot a few blocks from the Village Canvas, a small restaurant frequented by artists and art dealers. As he was walking down the street, he spotted a familiar face in front of the restaurant.

Altman stopped and stared. It was the Norwegian, the first Mr. Carpino, accompanied by sculptor Matthew Salazar. And someone else was with them. A woman. A woman with red hair and long legs. Altman felt sick at his stomach. The Norwegian bent down and kissed Shelley on the lips.

Anger replaced nausea, and Altman started toward the three people, but too late. They climbed into a Cadillac and drove away before he could reach them. The last he saw of Shelley, she was smoothing the Norwegian's black hair.

Altman drove slowly back to Brooklyn, his lunch plans forgotten. Shelley had left him for another man, and that man had compounded the insult by using him and his gallery to commit a crime. What a fool he'd been—too naïve and too greedy to see what was going on. Now, much too late, he saw what should have been obvious. Shelley knew as much about the gallery as he did, including everything about its expensive security system. He'd never felt like such an idiot. Not even the arching stones and steel cables of the Brooklyn Bridge could lift his spirits.

He didn't hear another word about the statue the rest of the day, but the next morning *The New York Times* carried a remarkable story. Winston Gardner, a spokesman for the Brooklyn Advancement Society, had announced the recovery of *The Spirit of Brooklyn*:

> "It was all an elaborate hoax," Mr. Gardner said. "We learned of a plot to steal the statue, so we engineered a theft of our own. We hid the statue in a place where no one would ever find it."
>
> Mr. Gardner told reporters that officials from the Brooklyn Advancement Society and the city of New York had been in complete control of the operation at all times. "No ransom was paid, and there was no damage to the statue," he said.

Altman found Mr. Gardner's remarks a little too self-congratulatory, especially in view of all those parts of the story he'd left out. Altman didn't know what to make of all this. He thought about calling the police or the district attorney or the newspapers. But what could he say? What exactly was the truth, and whom could he trust?

Then there was the embarrassment of the money he'd accepted from all those "customers." If a crime really had been committed, couldn't the money implicate him in that crime?

In addition to everything else, Altman was worried about his pride. He didn't want everyone in New York to know that a Norwegian "Carpino" had taken Shelley and made him the victim of a hoax at the same time.

So he finally decided not to call anyone. He paid his artists what he owed them, then used the rest of the money to buy himself out of his lease and move the gallery to Soho. Talented young artists soon began to seek him out, and before long he could count on a steady flow of real customers.

Shortly after moving to Soho, he received a telephone call from his old landlord in Flatbush. Someone had found a bunch of paintings in a rubbish heap in the alley—paintings by Rita Cordoba, Paul Angora, and a number of others. The landlord wondered what he should do with them.

"Just throw them away," Altman said. "They're worthless. It would be a crime to sell them."

⊙ ⊙ ⊙

One fall day about a year later, he drove over to Brooklyn Heights to discuss a sale with one of his new customers. The meeting ended with success, and he left in a relaxed mood. Standing on the sidewalk, he recalled his adventures of the previous year. In a moment of whimsy, he decided to look in on the statue. He'd sometimes wondered if it was a replica of the original. Mr. Gardner had given such a fictional account of the statue's recovery that anything seemed possible.

The Spirit of Brooklyn now stood in a small museum not far from the offices of the Brooklyn Advancement Society. It was late afternoon, and only a few people were waiting in line when Altman arrived. He moved along patiently, enjoying this break in his normal routine. When he reached the statue, he stood there several moments. He'd never really looked at it carefully, especially not on the morning it had magically appeared in his storeroom.

To get a closer look, he leaned across the velvet rope that separated the viewer from the statue. Something caught his eye, and he leaned farther, drawing the attention of one of the guards. "I'm sorry, sir," the guard said, "but I'll have to ask you not to get any closer to the statue."

Altman stood up and moved on, but not before he'd seen something few others would ever notice or care about, a tiny repair line on David's toe.

THE MAN
WHO FOUND
SAM

Sam Carter had a dark secret. This secret, if discovered, might offend many people, but the only one that Sam worried about was Kathy Halvorson, his wife.

While a graduate student at the University of Chicago, Sam had come across Mark Twain's review of *Outre-Mer*, a book in which Paul Bourget, a French novelist and essayist, had struggled to find the "American soul." Twain thought Bourget's book was a waste of ink, and he proceeded to tear it apart in an essay called "What Paul Bourget Thinks of Us," which appeared in the *North American Review* in 1895.

Sam's secret lay in the fact that he had written an article about the Twain-Bourget unpleasantness and an obscure literary journal had published it. The journal was cheaply printed and bound, and had a distribution of less than five hundred. The essay had never appeared online, and Sam prayed that Kathy would never see it. The article included these paragraphs:

> The trouble began when Twain, his words coated with irony, summarized Bourget's entire project. "M. Bourget would teach us to know ourselves;..." Twain wrote. "He would explain us to ourselves. Then we should understand ourselves; and after that be able to go on more intelligently."

> A few paragraphs later, another problem arose. Bourget had visited the United States, but had spent most of his time living amidst the upper-class resort society of Newport, Rhode Island. There, in Newport, Bourget wrote that "this 'American soul,' the principal interest and the great object of my voyage, appears behind the records of Newport for those who choose to see it."

> In response to this, Twain wrote that "I think M. Bourget meant to suggest that he expected to find the great 'American soul' secreted behind the ostentations

of Newport;..." This, of course, allowed Bourget to ignore millions of Americans who would never live in Newport because they lacked the money. Because of this financial reality, these people couldn't make any sort of contribution to Bourget's magical "American soul."

A few pages later, Twain summarized how Bourget made his observations and reached his conclusions. "Every now and then, at half-hour intervals, M. Bourget collects a hatful of airy inaccuracies and dissolves them in a panful of assorted abstractions,..."

At some point, Sam could've ended his article about Bourget and let the matter rest. Had he done that, he would not have had any reason to worry about a dark secret afterwards. But instead, he went on to chop up an essay written in defense of *Outre-Mer* by Paul Blouet, another French novelist and essayist, who used "Max O'Rell" as his pseudonym. Sam described the continued hostilities among Twain, Bourget, and O'Rell:

Finally, an American came to the aid of M. Bourget. Willa Cather roared out of Nebraska like a tornado and made some noticeably blunt statements about Mark Twain. Her article, dated May 5, 1895, appeared in the *Nebraska State Journal.* "Mr. Clemens did not like the book," she wrote, "and like all men of his class, and limited mentality, he cannot criticise [sic] without becoming personal and insulting."

Then there was even more from Ms. Cather: "He tried to demolish a serious and well considered work by publishing a scurrilous, slangy and loosely written article about it. In this article Mr. Clemens proves very little against Mr. Bourget and a very great deal against himself. He demonstrates clearly that he is neither a scholar, a reader or a man of letters and very little of a gentleman."

As mentioned above, Cather's article appeared in 1895. Nonetheless, ten years later, in 1905, Cather found herself at Delmonico's in New York City, where she and 169 others helped Mark Twain celebrate his seventieth birthday. The guests included William Dean Howells, Andrew Carnegie, Emily Post, and other luminaries.

By that time, Cather appears to have forgotten Twain's "scurrilous, slangy and loosely written" prose. In fact, it appears that she had forgotten all about M. Bourget and *Outre-Mer*. She had learned by then that it's better for a young writer's career if she can steer away from criticism of a certified literary genius like Mark Twain. She was no longer the defender of French visitors. She had become an agreeable lapdog.

Although Sam had written his account of the Twain-Bourget-O'Rell-Cather battle with complete sincerity, he hadn't anticipated that he might one day find himself married to someone who was on her way to becoming an authority on Cather's life and literary career. Kathy already knew about Bourget's book, Twain's article, and Cather's heated attack on Twain. But she apparently didn't know about Sam's article and its use of the word "lapdog." Why, Sam often asked himself, had he felt the need to use that insulting word? The only answer was that he, like Cather, had been young, and young writers are notoriously eager to begin publishing anything wherever they can, even if it requires an occasional overstatement.

◉ ◉ ◉

On a cold night in February, Sam began rereading the first volume of the *Autobiography of Mark Twain*, as published by the University of California Press. Although many readers had complained about the small type the publisher had chosen, Sam complained about nothing. He would've read the book with a microscope if necessary.

Kathy walked into the room, sat down at her computer, and said, "What are you reading, Sam?"

Sam, who was sitting in a rocking chair beside a floor lamp, looked up and said, "I'm rereading Twain's autobiography. By the time I finish, I hope I'll finally understand the real Sam Clemens. I've been rummaging around in his brain for years."

"Yes," Kathy said, "I know." She didn't say this sarcastically. She approved of her husband's obsession. She put her hands on the computer's keyboard and began rummaging around in the brain of Willa Cather.

Both Sam and Kathy taught in the department of English at the University of Southern Iowa in Delphi, a city on the banks of the Iowa River. The river had recently invaded the university's classroom buildings, museums, and auditoriums on the flood plain, buildings that long-departed administrators had chosen to erect there because they believed that a flood-control dam upstream would protect them forever. The river had flooded in 1993 and again in 2008, leaving everyone in the state with absolute faith that it would soon flood again.

Sam and Kathy were now teaching in an abandoned warehouse five miles from town, while the university demolished the flood-prone buildings and looked for appropriate locations for new buildings. The people of Delphi spoke about the flood problem *sotto voce*, given the fact that the state's population viewed the damage as the product of poor human judgment, not as the work of the Gods of rains and rivers. Or one could simply say that they blamed the university's administrators, not the residents of Mount Olympus.

But Sam and Kathy blamed no one. They had helped remove everything possible from the doomed English Cartography Building (ECB), and they now cheerfully rode the buses to and from the foul-smelling warehouse and taught their classes as best they could.

Sam and Kathy had no children, didn't want any, and knew how to prevent them. They thought of Mark Twain and Willa Cather as their children. They had conceived and given birth to Mark and Willa, and they intended to raise them in a way that would save them from the sentimental stuff of popular culture and the tedious ruminations of tenure-seeking boneheads.

"Kathy," Sam said. "I think I'm on to something. I don't know what it is, but I soon will."

"I'm sure you will," Kathy said. "Just be patient." Kathy often recommended patience for others and practiced it herself. Her friends and relatives thought it was one of her best qualities.

Sam and Kathy had chosen each other from a pool of about seven billion humans, approximately half being male and half being female. Sam had found that Kathy's appearance perfectly matched his deepest desires. She was five feet five inches tall, which was just right for Sam's five feet eight inches. The hair on her head was an attractive shade of blonde, which matched the color of her eyebrows, thereby proving to careful observers that Kathy's hair was naturally blonde and not the work of specialists in cosmetology and hair design.

Kathy's face formed a perfectly symmetrical oval. Her complexion was a gentle pale and free of any distracting marks. But the most memorable aspect of her face was her eyes, which were greener than the greenest leaves on any tree in Wisconsin, Minnesota, or Ontario. Other states and provinces also had green leaves, but Sam hadn't yet had the time or money to examine all the trees in all those places.

Sam had also noticed another physical attribute that held special importance for him. Kathy had beautiful legs, both of which surpassed what Sam had observed to be the common standard among the female academicians in the English Cartography Building.

Kathy had grown up on a farm in Minnesota, where she had discovered that she could easily jump the three strands of the average barbed-wire fence. When she enrolled in junior high school, the girls' track coach expressed astonishment at the speed with which Kathy could run the hurdles. She never knocked a hurdle over and never lost a race. During her six years of junior and senior high school, she won the state championship for her age group every year and set records that were unlikely to ever be broken.

By the time Sam met Kathy, she was running a different kind of race. She published something of importance every year and expected to become a full professor before her twenty-eighth birthday. Sam loved everything about her, including foremost her intellect and her legs. If forced to choose between the two, Sam would've found the choice impossible. After searching without success for the Becky Thatcher of his world, he had fallen for Kathy, or perhaps Kathy was his Becky Thatcher.

For her part, Kathy had looked carefully at Sam's entry in the Delphi spouse competition. His brown hair, brown eyes, and dark complexion met her requirements, but she was most impressed by his personality. He never got angry, never grew impatient, and never used the vulgarities commonly heard in barnyards and pool halls. "Dern the dern fog" was his most forceful expression. Kathy knew that she was a better teacher and scholar than Sam, but she didn't care and neither did he.

Sam had never excelled at any sport. Prior to college, he never did well in any subject but reading. From K through 12, he was consistently average. Regardless of what assignments his teachers gave him, he spent his time reading and rereading the works of Mark Twain. He read slowly and carefully, and rejected all attempts to teach him speed reading. When he reached the age of puberty, he had wet dreams about Becky Thatcher. He succeeded in academia because he knew everything about Mark Twain. His Ph.D. dissertation was as good as it needed to be, primarily because the University of California had given him early access to Twain's correspondence.

Both Sam and Kathy were quite frugal. Sam never wasted money on the electronic gadgets that millions of men found essential for their happiness. His wardrobe was a study in moderation: he owned one suit, one sport coat, five pairs of pants, five shirts, five ties, five pairs of socks, and two pairs of shoes. For casual wear, he owned two pairs of khaki pants, one pair of walking shoes, and assorted shirts and socks too worn out for classroom use. He wasted money only on books, which, for an assistant professor of English, wasn't really wasteful.

◉ ◉ ◉

A week prior to spring break, Sam mentioned to Kathy that he'd like to spend a day or two in Hannibal, Missouri, in hopes of resurrecting something of Mark Twain's personality, honesty, and literary greatness. In his opinion, English professors all over the world had analyzed Twain's work until they had wrung it dry of its brooding anger and turned it into a stack of textbooks similar to those used to teach accounting. Sam and Kathy had visited Hannibal many times before, but the place always deserved another look.

In order to make the trip, they would need a car, one of the many extravagant objects they had learned they didn't need, provided they could find alternatives. In this case, Wilson's Easy Come & Easy Go supplied all their automotive needs. They, their luggage, and their picnic basket arrived by Red Star Cab at Wilson's address on Riverside Drive on Monday morning.

"Sam, Kathy," Wilson boomed as they walked into his small office, the walls of which were covered with photos of eight-cylinder cars built decades before when the price of gasoline was twenty-five cents a gallon. The cars were large, and so was Wilson. "I've got a nice Pontiac Catalina for you. Ignore the rust and listen to the engine. It'll take you to hell and back if you want it to."

"We were thinking of a leisurely drive to Hannibal, Missouri," Sam said.

"Hell can wait," Kathy said. "We want to drive down before the floods begin."

"A wise precaution," Wilson said, "very wise. This baby cruises at a hundred and twenty, but you have to watch out for the troopers in Missouri. They love to give tickets to anyone with out-of-state plates."

"As I said," Sam said politely. "We plan on a leisurely drive."

"Oh, sure. Oh, sure," Wilson said. "Take your time. Take your time. That'll be forty dollars a day plus tax. You buy the gas. You really need the high-octane stuff they don't sell anymore. The engine will knock like hell sometimes, but what can you do?"

"We'll manage," Kathy said.

"The keys are in the car. Have a nice trip."

"I'm sure we will," Sam said.

They put their things into the trunk, Sam closed the lid, and Kathy seated herself behind the steering wheel. Neither she nor Sam liked to drive, but they had reached an agreement a few years before. She would drive first, and Sam would drive later, after he was fully awake. It would take four or five hours for him to reach the wakefulness required for the operation of Pontiacs, bulldozers, and other heavy equipment.

In order to drive from Delphi to Hannibal by the shortest route, one has to take the Avenue of the Saints, a four-lane highway from Saint Paul to Saint Louis. Although Sam and Kathy thought the Avenue of the Saints was a waste of farmland, it delivered them, nonetheless, into the west end of Hannibal, where they had reserved a room at the Tom Sawyer Hotel, which stood across the street from the Huck Finn Hotel. Sam parked the Pontiac under the ugly portico, and Kathy went into the ugly lobby to register.

An hour later, they walked into the dining room, followed the hostess to their table, and ordered vodka martinis. Then they turned to the artery-clogging entrées on the menu. Both of them rejected the deep-fried catfish, deep-fried scallops, and deep-fried shrimp. They rejected all beef, pork, lamb, and any kind of meat that had been ground up and put back together. By common agreement, Sam gave their order to the waiter. He did this because he could talk faster than Kathy and he was a native of Missouri, a state in which fast talkers won the most competitive events.

"Our special today," the waiter said rapidly, "is deep-fried catfish with French fries and your choice of cottage cheese or coleslaw." The waiter was tall, slim, and too good-looking to ever do anything important.

"No deep-fried food, please," Sam said. "We'd both like salmon seared in a pan with olive oil. No cheese of any kind. Do you have any vegetables?"

"I think we have green beans." The waiter's uncertainty about this topic caused him to speak more slowly than usual.

"That's good enough. We'd like them steamed and not over-cooked."

The food, when it finally arrived, was neither good nor nutritious. Sam and Kathy had hoped for a miracle but had received tourist food at tourist prices. After they'd eaten as much as they could stand, Kathy said, "I think that for the rest of the trip we should eat only the food we brought along."

"Agreed," Sam said. He and Kathy agreed on just about everything. Wherever they went, on campus or far away, Sam and Kathy appeared to be a perfect couple. For the most part, that observation was accurate. But Sam's dark secret lurked behind everything he said or did.

⊚ ⊚ ⊚

The next afternoon, Kathy drove them down to the part of Hannibal that the city fathers and mothers had saved for the town's tourist trade. Here, Sam and Kathy visited what was officially labeled the Mark Twain Boyhood Home, a small two-story frame house with white clapboard siding and gray shingles. The front of the house displayed two windows on the first floor and three on the second. Each of these had a green window box where flowers bloomed during the spring and summer. But Sam and Kathy had arrived too early for flowers. They eventually reached the exit from the Mark Twain Boyhood Home, which led them directly into a bookstore in the white-limestone house next door. Even though they liked bookstores, they didn't need any duplicates of Twain's books and made no purchases.

They also toured the Becky Thatcher House, the J.M. Clemens Justice of the Peace Office, Grant's Drug Store, and two museums. In all these places, as in the Twain house, they found themselves surrounded by hoards of schoolchildren who ran everywhere they went, with no regard for the elderly, infirm, or anyone else. Finally, with night coming on, Sam and Kathy escaped to the top of the levee and peered at the eternal waters of the Mississippi River. Fog was gathering over the water.

Sam pointed back at the streets they'd just abandoned. "The trouble with all those buildings," he said, "is that they discourage any attempts to reflect on the real life of Sam Clemens. Maybe it's just the kids. They've been eating too much sugar and not enough broccoli."

A small riverboat with twin diesel engines and a *faux* stern wheel came downriver with a load of tourists as a man's voice recited a narrative about Mark Twain's brief career as a riverboat pilot. As the boat puttered along, an orange, yellow, and black Burlington Northern Santa Fe locomotive pulled a line of grain cars along the tracks at the bottom of the levee.

A few yards from Sam and Kathy, an old man stood in the grass, smoking a cigar. After the train had passed, Sam walked over to this man while Kathy went on down the levee, crossed the tracks, walked around a fenced parking lot, crossed another set of tracks, and stopped at the river.

"Those kids you were talking about will drive you crazy," the man said to Sam. "I used to work in one of the shops. When a herd of the little bastards came through, I wanted to drown them."

"You have all my sympathy," Sam said. "What do you do now?"

"I'm retired, surviving on social security and a small pension. My brother and I share a little house. If the cost of everything keeps going up, we'll have to apply for food stamps."

"Do you like Mark Twain's books?" Sam said.

"Sure," the man said. "I like his honesty. He wrote a lot of things that some people choose to ignore. Did you, for example, see a building in this town named after Jim? All that people want is Tom, Becky, and Huck. That's what attracts the tourist money."

"We came here because we're trying to find the real Sam Clemens," Sam said.

"You came to the wrong place," the man said, looking tolerantly at Sam. "You won't learn anything here that you can't find in a good library. That's where you'll find the real Sam Clemens." The man scratched his gray mustache. "I can't tell you any more than that. Talk to your wife. She's smarter than you. Tell her the truth. Tell her what you really think." He took out his pocket watch and looked at it. "I have to go," he said. "Good luck."

"Thanks," Sam said. He watched the man walk to the top of the levee and disappear down the other side.

Sam turned and watched Kathy walk away from the river and back to where he stood. "I guess that old man told me everything I'll find here," he said. "I was hoping for an epiphany. But I haven't had one."

"What old man?" Kathy said.

Sam looked at her. "The man I was talking to. Didn't you see him?"

"No." Kathy didn't say anything else. Sam sometimes saw things she didn't.

Sam hesitated. "I have to tell you something," he said. "I wrote an article about Mark Twain and Willa Cather when I was in grad school. It's highly critical of Cather. You might not like it. It might make you angry."

"Sam," Kathy said, "I read that article two days after arriving in Delphi. Everyone in the ECB has read it, including the cartographers. It's required reading for all members of the English faculty. Everyone loves it."

"Do you mean it didn't offend you?"

"Of course not. Cather was full of contradictions. That's one of the things I like about her. She got angry about things that she later thought were of no importance. Most great writers are like that. Haven't you found contradictions in Twain's work?"

"Dozens of them. There may be hundreds."

"Does it make you angry that I just asked that question?"

"Of course not."

"Good. Let's have a picnic."

"Where? Here?"

"No," she said. "It's too cold, and it's getting dark. We'll find what we need in the picnic basket and have the picnic in our room. All we need to buy is a bottle of champagne."

"I think we can find one," Sam said. "You can find anything you want in Missouri."

"Good," Kathy said. She looked back at the Mississippi. "It's getting really foggy on the river," she said. "Can you still see the opposite shore?"

Sam looked at the river. "No," he said. "I couldn't promise you that Illinois is still there, although there's a statistical probability that it is." They stood together, holding hands, watching the river. The tourist boat had disappeared, and a towboat had come into view, pushing its fifteen barges slowly up the main channel.

"I can't see much of anything," Kathy said.

"Me neither. I can barely see the running lights on those barges."

"We'd better go."

"Could we stay just a few more minutes?" Sam said.

"Okay," Kathy said.

"Jim and Huck missed the Ohio River on a night like this."

"I remember."

They watched the barges until they disappeared. Then Sam turned toward Kathy, placed his hand on her cheek, and whispered. "Dern the dern fog," he said.

GOODLOVE

My failures with women have all followed the same script. Four college students, five graduate students, and seven lawyers have all dumped me faster than the laws of physics should allow. I married one of these women. She had the legs of a goddess and the personality of a volcano. Her final eruption occurred in divorce court, where she relieved me of more money than a high-school teacher can afford to lose.

Faced with a life of celibacy and drunkenness, I joined GoodLove.com in desperation and with little hope of finding the "soul mate" that this computer dating service promised. I wanted a woman who was both attractive and financially independent, and I knew how difficult it would be to find her. Nonetheless, I sent my credit-card number to GoodLove.com, along with instructions to sign me up for three months and make it snappy.

GoodLove.com responded with electronic speed, first sucking one hundred dollars from my credit-card account and then sending me a million gigabytes of forms to fill out, including what this gang of bandits called "My Autobiography."

I went straight to work on this document, which began with a description of my physical self. My real physical self had never captured the hearts of females from my real past. So I made up a description that seemed more appealing. I said I was thirty years old, six feet two, and as strong as a horse. This last detail would, I assumed, imply to my future sweetheart that I was also as well endowed as a horse in one of its crucial anatomical dimensions.

Next I made up my personal history. I was, I revealed, as wealthy as the late John D. Rockefeller. I owned all the gold mines in Africa and all the pay toilets in North America. I also owned all the payday-loan shops in New York, New Jersey, and Florida; and I had just acquired a 51 percent share of Berkshire Hathaway and all the corporations in Denmark. I gave myself the name GotToHaveYou624.

Finally, because my face lacked the refinements needed to attract women with good eyesight, I substituted a photograph of Paul Newman taken when he was twenty-one years old and still as strong as a horse.

I sent this fiction to GoodLove.com, along with a thousand other forms and affidavits. Having done all this, my mood began to improve. With visions of Ms. Right writhing in my brain like a Babylonian harlot, I spent the evening with a copy of *Great Expectations*. I was a gentleman and had no need to waste my time grading American history exams completed by the brats at Bob Feller High School in Cleveland. I would soon marry money and raise a family. I had learned that success required no more than a confident exterior and a lifetime supply of sliced baloney.

The morning after my enrollment in GoodLove.com, five hundred messages had landed in my computer-dating email account. I looked at the pictures of all the women who had sent the emails and picked the one that stimulated my libido the most. She had called herself LoveMeTender8876. "I love you already," she wrote. "You've accomplished so much in your young life, and your intellectual gifts are so apparent. I want to ride behind you on your Harley, with my arms wrapped around you in a loving embrace. Please write back as soon as you can."

This gorgeous 24-year-old woman had assumed that I owned a Harley-Davidson motorcycle, a fabrication that I would have included in My Autobiography if I'd thought of it. I made a note to add that detail when I found the time, although it didn't seem to matter all that much. It had apparently made no difference to LoveMeTender8876, who had assumed that the owner of all the pay toilets in North America would naturally have dozens of Harleys in his stable.

"Dear LoveMeTender8876," I wrote. "I love you, too. How much money do you have?"

This message elicited a short response. "Dear GotToHaveY-ou624," she wrote. "I have $48.13."

I clicked the refuse-all-mail button and went back to the other 499 emails. This time I read the My Autobiography data attached to the picture of a lovely 28-year-old woman from Peoria, Illinois. This sentence caught my attention: "I recently inherited eight million dollars." This woman had labeled herself GimmeGimme2492.

I responded with an invitation for her to meet me in the café at the BP-Disaster Truck Stop on I-80 in Gary, Indiana, where she appeared the next afternoon. This blond-haired, significantly breasted woman looked exactly like the photograph for GimmeGimme2492. I looked nothing like the youthful Paul Newman. "Hi, GimmeGimme," I said. "I'm GotToHaveYou."

"What?" she said. "How old are you?"

"Thirty."

"You don't look it. How tall are you?"

"Five-six."

"Your autobiography said you were six-two. How many pay toilets do you own?"

"Actually, none."

"You lying bastard," she screamed.

All the other patrons in the room froze like *The Burghers of Calais*. Everyone looked at GimmeGimme2492, who responded with a flood of words that were never sacred and always profane. She charged out of the room, pausing along the way to destroy one cash register, two glass doors, and three hundred heavy-duty dinner plates. I was heading for the exit when the commanding voice of the manager rose from the silence of the other *Burghers*. "Just a minute, mister. Who's going to pay for all this damage your girlfriend left behind?"

"I will," I said, my authoritative voice now restored. "Here's my credit card." I handed him a card I'd found at Gary's Greyhound Bus Depot that morning.

The manager wrote down all the data he needed and returned the card. "Here you go, Mister Astor. Don't call again, and don't have a nice day."

"Same to you," I said, offended by the man's tone. I caught the next bus back to Cleveland and began grading the stack of exams.

◉ ◉ ◉

I spent the better part of the next day arguing with students about their grades on the exam. Many of them refused to accept the fact that the Mexican War and the Spanish-American War were actually two different events at two different times and that only one of those wars had inspired people to race around the countryside shouting "Remember the Alamo."

By the end of the day, all this discord had caused me to think again of GoodLove.com and my desire to obtain both a wife and her money. My first attempts had failed. I needed a new strategy.

This time I took a more subtle approach. I selected my next candidate by finding the photographs of reasonably attractive women and reading the employment information in their My Autobiographies. This led me to a middle-aged woman who said she was a vice president of JCMorgan Chase. Her name was DiversifiedLove$$$.

I began by sending her a "Silicon Kiss," which was another one of GoodLove.com's inventions. By clicking the appropriate button, I caused the message "You've Been Kissed" to appear at the GoodLove.com account belonging to DiversifiedLove$$$. She then replied by sending me an email message, which said, among other things, "You must be an idiot if you think I'd be interested in a guy whose income depends on the receipts from pay toilets. I'd advise you, at your earliest convenience, to drown yourself in the Cuyahoga River. This conversation is over."

This VP of JCMorgan Chase knew the geography of Cleveland, but she lacked the personality attributes required for finding a long-term relationship at GoodLove.com. I wanted to explain this to her, but she'd already clicked the button that blocked all future messages from me to her.

This experience left me feeling hopeless and abandoned. I thought about drowning myself in either the Cuyahoga River or Lake Erie, but I didn't want to give DiversifiedLove$$$ the pleasure I knew this would bring her. So I got out a bottle of Templeton Rye and drank myself to sleep.

◉ ◉ ◉

The next morning, I called the principal's office and said that I was deathly ill and couldn't possibly begin teaching my students about the invention of the cotton gin, the institution of slavery, and all the other causes that led to the Civil War. I spoke the truth when I said how sick I was, but I left out the part about the Templeton Rye. I knew that the substitute teacher who would take my place for the day would know nothing about the causes of the Civil War and that my students would regress to the level of the hominids of the Lower Paleolithic Period and begin throwing each other out the third-floor windows. This saddened me, but I had to deal with the trio of baritone saxophones roaring in my head.

By three o'clock in the afternoon, I could walk upright and move from room to room, making sounds that resembled human speech. The idea of food never invaded my mind, but I began drinking soda water from a gallon jug. By five o'clock, I had figured out how to turn on my computer, and two hours later I had entered the domain of GoodLove.com.

I recalled that the next day was Saturday, and that I could spend an entire weekend searching for the solution to all my problems. This time, reality would guide my efforts. I would know the truth and it would set me free. I ignored all photo-

156

graphs of young, beautiful women and searched for wealthy widows of my own age or older. Templeton Rye had purged me of all desire for sexual congress. All I wanted now was wealth and respectability. I would even forego respectability, if necessary, in order to make an early escape from Bob Feller High School.

One week later, I receive an email from GloriaB625. "Dear GotToHaveYou624," she wrote. "I require the presence of an educated man to accompany me to various social and philanthropic events in Cleveland and its suburbs. He must be intelligent, well-read, and capable of knowing when to keep his mouth shut. My investigators have learned that you are a skilled schoolteacher at Bob Feller High School. They also learned that you drink too much, but that doesn't interest me at present. I will be available to interview you at my residence in Shaker Heights next Wednesday, immediately after you complete your teaching duties for the day. My driver will meet you in the parking lot directly east of the school. Look for a black Mercedes-Benz, and don't keep the driver waiting."

I didn't keep him waiting. He opened the back door, I got in, and we drove to a mansion slightly smaller than your average aircraft carrier. The butler, Mr. Overstreet, showed me into a walnut-paneled office, where a slender brown-haired woman in a black dress sat behind a spotless desk. She motioned toward a chair and waited for me to sit down. I immediately saw that I should demonstrate my ability to keep my mouth shut. I estimated that the woman was about seventy years old, fifteen years older than I.

"Mister Nolan," she said, "I am the widow of the late Chesterfield Biltmore. I manage my husband's business and oversee the activities of his charitable foundation, which provides grants for schools, colleges, and universities. I need you to travel with me and attend various functions. If you can handle this in an appropriate manner, I will support you for the rest of my life and provide a generous annuity for you thereafter. An event is scheduled for Saturday night. If you can perform your duties adequately, I will offer you a contract. Do you wish to attend this event?"

This was clearly an appropriate time to speak. "Yes," I said.

"My driver will take you to a men's shop where you can obtain the required evening wear. Good day."

I stood up. "Good day," I said. Then I turned and walked out.

While on the way to the men's shop, I asked the driver the appropriate form of address for Mrs. Biltmore. "Missus Biltmore," he said. Those were the first and last words he said to me that day. He had learned when to keep his mouth shut.

◉ ◉ ◉

On Saturday evening at eight o'clock, I arrived at the mansion in black tie and all the other appropriate duds. At eight-thirty, we departed for the bacchanalia at the Terminal Tower, a 52-story Beaux-Arts building that stood above the Cleveland Union

Terminal, which had opened for business just in time to receive the great streamliners of the 1930s through the 1950s.

Our event took place in a large and expensively appointed room on the thirty-ninth floor, a spot reserved for citizens who occupied the highest income-tax brackets. Before the evening ended, various eager informants had taken me aside to point out that the Biltmore family had originally made its fortune in railroads and real estate during the nineteenth century, facts already known by every literate resident of Cleveland.

Mrs. Biltmore and I wandered here and there, stopping to talk to those attendees that Mrs. B wanted to talk to. In response to a question from an elderly gentleman, I agreed that what the city's schools needed most was strict discipline, clearly stated rules, and rigorous enforcement thereof. Five minutes later, I agreed with another elderly gentleman, who believed that the schools had codes of conduct that were far too strict and that more freedom would bring out the inherent creativity that all children possessed.

I followed Mrs. B from one spot to another, speaking only when spoken to and obtaining vodka martinis only when Mrs. B allowed me to do so. When we reached a young woman with blond hair that billowed like the sails on the Pequod, Mrs. B spoke to her at length, but used her elbow to move me to a more-distant location when I drifted within six inches of the blond angel, an angel I would have liked to keep within arm's reach for eternity or longer, depending on the exact nature of eternity.

When we stopped to chat with a woman whose face had been lifted more times than the hoist at your local auto-repair shop, Mrs. B noted a growing lust in the woman's green eyes and sent me off to write a 5000-word history of Cleveland's public schools, a job that would require several days and an un-limited supply of vodka martinis. By the time I returned to ask Mrs. B for a mainframe computer, the green-eyed woman had cornered someone else, and Mrs. B said she no longer needed the five thousand words.

By midnight, I was so exhausted that I gladly rode back to the mansion with Mrs. B and followed the butler to a bedroom reserved for only me. I took off the duds, threw them on the floor, and lay down on the bed, where I slept for the next twelve hours, during which I had recurring dreams of billowing blond hair, Beaux-Arts buildings, and an endless prohibition of vodka martinis.

⊛ ⊛ ⊛

Early the next afternoon, Mrs. B summoned me to her office. She motioned toward the usual chair and I took it. "Mr. Nolan," she said, "your performance at last night's event, though marked by a few flaws, was adequate." She spoke while looking to one side, which struck me as rude until I looked in the same direc-tion. A mirror on the wall to her left gave her a perfect view of my right profile. I never learned why she wanted to observe my profile or if she used the mirror on everyone.

"If you accept my offer, you'll receive the monetary benefits I mentioned during our first interview. This position will require you to resign from your teaching job and change your residence from your current apartment to this house. The room you slept in last night will be yours to keep. You'll be given time off to visit friends and relatives, but for the most part you'll have to remain in this house for whatever needs I may have." She turned and looked directly into my eyes. "Those needs will include tasks I do not wish to specify at present. Your reward for all this will be financial security for the rest of your life. After my death, you'll have the money to live anywhere on earth that suits you. Think it over. If you accept this offer, your duties will begin immediately. This will inconvenience the administration at the Bob Feller High School, but I'll contact the superintendent of schools and make the transition acceptable to everyone. Think it over and give me your decision by five o'clock this afternoon."

I thought it over. The financial rewards would be more than I'd ever dreamt of, but the loss of freedom would make life more difficult than it already was. After Mrs. B died, I'd have complete freedom, but what if she lived longer than I did? She was older than I, but women live longer than men. She might easily outlive me.

At five o'clock, I gave Mrs. Biltmore my decision. Then I went to my apartment to get ready for the rest of my life. On

Monday morning, I began the day with this question: "How," I asked, "did Reconstruction fail to accomplish the goals of the Civil War?"

⊚ ⊚ ⊚

One Saturday afternoon about a year later, I decided to drive past the mansion that I had rejected in favor of freedom, if the life of a teacher can honestly be called free. I intended to park in the driveway and take a long look at the house, but Howard Grover, Mrs. B's gardener, had blocked the view with his truck. When he recognized me, he waved and walked over to my old Chevy. "Howard," I said after rolling down the window, "how are the yards and gardens at the Biltmore mansion?"

They're just fine, but it's all kind of sad now that Missus Biltmore is gone."

"Gone?" I said. "What do you mean?"

"Missus Biltmore died about a month ago. Didn't you know? It was in all the papers and on TV."

"I guess I missed it," I said, looking away to hide my embarrassment.

"I guess you did."

"How did she die?" I said, looking back at Howard.

"You'd better talk to Mister Overstreet about that," he said. "He knows all about it. He's in the house. I'll move the truck out of your way."

If Mr. Overstreet was surprised to see me, he didn't show it. He was dressed in khaki pants and a sport shirt instead of the black suit he usually wore. Piles of boxes stood in the foyer. "Missus Biltmore died of cancer," he said. "It didn't come as a surprise. She'd confided in me almost two years ago. She told no one else until the last week. All of us who worked here were with her at the end. She had no one else." He looked at me rather sternly as he made this last statement.

"But she was famous in this city," I said. "Hundreds of people would have come to see her."

"Those people knew her because of her money. She had no one else who cared for her as a human being. She was extremely kind and generous to us. She treated us as equals, and we therefore loved her. She wanted someone else, a friend instead of an employee, someone she could talk to about life's great mysteries, but she never found anyone like that."

"If only I'd known."

"Yes, if only you had. And you would have known if you had accepted her offer. But neither she nor I would have told you before that acceptance. That would have given you a reason to stay here, but only because of a material reward that you knew would soon become yours."

"What will all of you do?" I said, eager to change the subject from me to anyone else.

"Missus Biltmore has provided generously for all of us. The bulk of her estate will go to the Biltmore Educational Foundation, but the cook, the two maids, the driver, the gardener, and will all be well provided for. We've all been here for decades, and we can all now retire."

And I cannot, I said to myself. "Thank you, Mister Overstreet," I finally said.

"You're very welcome," he said. "If you have no more questions, I'll get back to work. We're getting the house and grounds ready for sale."

"You've answered all my questions," I said. "I'll go now." I walked outside, got into my car, and drove away. I didn't intend to look back, but I did, one last time.

WAR

AND

PEACE

Luke and Natalie met each other at the intersection of Lexington and Dover streets on a warm night early in May. They and hundreds of other people had sat down in the street and refused to move. They would end this exercise, they said, when the war ended.

While waiting for the authorities to employ whatever act of violence they intended, Luke and Natalie began to talk.

Both said they were pacifists, although Natalie confessed that she had once thrown a copy of *War and Peace* at a man who wouldn't leave her alone.

The police began lobbing tear gas canisters toward the intersection, although those canisters rarely landed anywhere near the protesters. When the police finally began hitting the target, Luke and Natalie coughed together, ran together, and spent the night together.

Luke lived in a four-story brick building that had once been a railroad hotel. This building and the tavern beside it stood across the street from the Rock Island Depot. The noise from the trains sometimes woke the other residents of the old hotel, but not Luke. He'd spent his childhood near railroads in Nebraska.

That night, Luke and Natalie did something more pleasurable than sitting in the street. "You can come in now," she said after the preliminaries. Luke had never heard anyone say it that way before, but Natalie was more cosmopolitan than he. She came from New York. He came from Nebraska.

At three o'clock in the morning, Natalie shook Luke's shoulder and said, "Don't these trains ever stop?"

Luke rolled over and said, "No, they never stop. That's the nature of railroads."

"Do you have a car?" she said.

"Yes."

"Then take me home."

"There's a curfew. The police will arrest us."

They didn't leave Luke's apartment that night, but in a couple of weeks, Natalie had grown accustomed to the bells and whistles of the Chicago, Rock Island, and Pacific Railroad. In the middle of May, she moved in.

The next Sunday, they walked along the tracks to the river, where they watched the water for several minutes. "Do you want to walk across the bridge?" Natalie said.

"You're kidding," Luke said. "What if a train comes along?"

"They always slow down by the time they reach the bridge. We can beat it to the other side if we hear one coming."

"You go first."

Natalie started across the bridge, and Luke followed. They walked on the best surface available, the ties that supported the rails. A steel superstructure held the bridge up, but it stood under the ties, not beside them. After walking about twenty feet, Luke looked down between the ties and wished he'd never begun anything this suicidal. Far below, the river twirled and eddied, still bank full with melt water from Minnesota. Luke felt lightheaded. He looked up and breathed deeply several times. Then he looked at Natalie, who was chugging toward the opposite shore. "Natalie," Luke said. "I'm going back. I hope I can make it."

She turned and looked at him. "Walk slowly," she said, "and don't look down. I'm coming."

Luke followed these instructions, Natalie caught up with him before he reached the shore. "You didn't tell me you suffered from vertigo," she said.

"It was a test," he said. "I thought I'd outgrown it."

"The next time you want a test, go to a tall building and look down from a window on the top floor. Don't walk across a railroad bridge."

They walked away from the bridge and down the embankment, where they found a quiet place in a grove of young maple trees. They lay down and talked for a long time. Finally, Luke said, "Thanks for saving me on the bridge. I love you."

"I love you, too," Natalie said. "But I have to tell you something. There's someone else."

"Get rid of him. I'm much better."

Natalie laughed. "You're good," she said.

They climbed up the embankment and walked back to the depot. A century before, Irish immigrants had built it with locally made bricks, using red for the bottom half of each wall and blonde for the top. Semaphore signals stood in front of the building. An ancient baggage cart with steel wheels and a wooden deck sat on the brick platform. Inside the depot, seated at his bay window, the agent was writing train orders.

Luke and Natalie turned and walked down Cedar Street to the A&P. Both of them claimed to be vegetarians, but they cheated and bought salmon. "It's good for you," Natalie said. After walking back to Luke's apartment, they cooked their lunch, ate slowly, and got undressed for a nap.

Luke watched Natalie as she took off her clothes. She had delicate features, with eyes that were somewhere between gray and blue. Her skin looked as pale as white porcelain, and her hair was as dark as black onyx. She had long slender legs, not sculptured like Tina Turner's, but still beautiful.

◎ ◎ ◎

Early in June, Luke found a summer job with the city street crew, running a jackhammer and laying asphalt. Work started at 7:00 AM and ended at 3:30. Natalie didn't look for a job. She said she had enough money to make it through the summer. In Luke's absence, she went to the university library or got together with three friends—Tessa, Scarlet, and Mary. In the evenings, Luke and Natalie reported their activities for the day, expanding them into heroic adventures. Then they laughed at how clever they were. When the summer ended, they became students again.

That fall, the Rock Island ran its last passenger train through town. Two hours before it arrived, Natalie's friends descended on the apartment. They wanted to board the last train and get off at the next stop. This trip required someone with a car. Luke would have to drive to East Liberty to pick up the survivors and bring them back. "Maybe you want to take the train yourself," Tessa said.

"That's okay," Luke said. "I've taken enough trains for one lifetime." Both of Luke's parents had worked as depot agents for the Burlington Railroad as he grew up. Natalie and the three friends climbed onto the train and Luke drove his 1956 Chevy down Highway 6, arriving in East Liberty just minutes behind the train. That night, they sat in Luke's apartment and drank red wine in honor of the Rock Island's red and black diesel locomotives.

Fall ended and winter arrived with a freezing blast out of Nebraska. Natalie showed Luke her new coat, which the maker had blessed with all the latest technology in coat design. Luke still wore his old coat, which required much repair work on long winter nights. Both Natalie and Luke owned the best in caps and gloves.

Every day Luke and Natalie walked several blocks north to campus. Both had chosen to major in English, and most of their classes met in the Hall of Liberal Arts, a massive Beaux-Arts building constructed with white limestone. Each of them planned to graduate in the spring, at a time when college graduates could still find jobs.

Graduation day arrived with its usual platitudes. The commencement speaker reminded everyone that this was a beginning, not an ending. The graduates paid little attention to the speech. Luke thought about the salary he'd earn. Natalie thought of other things.

Afterwords, Luke and Natalie briefly escaped from their parents. "I'll call you after I get to Chicago," Luke said.

"Good," Natalie said, "but do you remember what I said about someone else?"

Luke felt a knot of fear in his stomach. "Yes," he said, "and I'm still better than he is."

Natalie didn't laugh. "It's a *she*, Luke. We've been talking about it for months, and I've finally decided. I'm sorry."

"Who is it?" he managed to say.

"Tessa."

Luke felt stunned. It made no difference that Natalie had dumped him for a woman instead of a man. That didn't make it any easier.

He knew he'd get over it. He'd find someone else. He moved to Chicago and started his new job. He had to support himself, which meant that he had to impress his boss, and his boss wouldn't care about Natalie and Tessa.

Many years later, the war finally ended. At work and on the Howard Street elevated line that took him to and from his job, it seemed to Luke that no one had noticed.

EASY
REST

On his sixty-ninth birthday, Bob Springer moved into the Easy Rest Retirement Village. His immediate complaint was that all the other residents were old. They looked old, smelled old, and were old. The majority of them were younger than Bob, but he refused to admit that he was old in any way. Everything about his fellow residents depressed him. In his opinion, they would've been better off dead.

Bob had rejected almost all attempts by the management to engage him in group activities such as bingo, ballroom dancing, or barbershop quartets. He had, on just one occasion, agreed to join twenty of his fellow retirees for a walk along the edge of a nearby bluff, where he and the others could enjoy a view of the Mississippi River, with its driftwood, sandbars, and long narrow islands. But Bob quickly lost interest in this sport. He preferred to observe nature on the screen of his sixty-inch television set.

Then Millie moved in.

Millie did not announce her age to the other old folks, but Bob guessed it to be about fifty-five, the minimum age required for admission to the Easy Rest Retirement Village. Otherwise, he would've thought her to be around thirty. Millie dyed her hair red, wore short skirts, and displayed the kind of legs that drove men and boys to do things that would cause hair to grow on their palms.

Millie gave Bob the motivation to interact with someone. And when he learned that she was addicted to the books of P.G. Wodehouse, he drove his Ford Fiesta ten miles to Dubuque and bought a copy of *Money for Nothing* from the Prairie Flower Bookstore.

Bob got ready to impress Millie with his best features—rugged good looks, a convincing smile, and a baritone voice that had made him rich during his long career as an actor in television commercials. Sadly, Bob had lost his fortune speculating on the stock market. This had forced him to leave the Upper East Side of Manhattan and move back to the Middle West, first to Joliet, then to Peoria, and finally to the Easy Rest in northeast Iowa.

The village occupied a four-story, U-shaped building like those that stood along the Howard Street elevated tracks in Chicago.

Three days after he bought the book, Bob arranged his movements so that he'd run into Millie as he walked down the hallway toward the barbershop. "Hello," he said, "how nice to see a new resident. I'm Bob, Bob Springer."

"I'm happy to meet you," she said. "I'm Millie Busch."

"I just finished reading *Money for Nothing*," Bob said. "Very entertaining." He hadn't actually read the book, but he'd memorized the title.

"My, my," she said. "I didn't know anyone here read Wodehouse."

"Oh sure," Bob said. "I've been a fan of his for years."

"We'll have to chat about his work sometime. Perhaps over tea."

Bob hated tea. "Absolutely," he said. "Absolutely."

A few days later, Bob met Millie at the Wee Cup Tea Shoppe one afternoon. The walls, woodwork, and pastry cases were covered with water-color paintings, all of which had been created by the residents. Their work displayed one-room schools, Christmas trees, jack-o-lanterns, and similar wholesome objects. "Wodehouse would've loved this place," Millie said. "It would've inspired endless parodies."

Bob had forgotten the meaning of "parodies." Nonetheless, he said, "Absolutely."

Millie put a copy of *Very Good, Jeeves!* on the table. "Don't you just love Jeeves and Wooster?" she said.

"Yes. Love them."

"I've been rereading this book."

"One of my favorite novels," Bob said.

Millie hesitated. "It's a collection of short stories," she said.

"Oh," Bob said. "I must have it confused with another book. There are so many of them, almost a hundred." Bob's research on Wodehouse had begun and ended with the dust jacket for *Money for Nothing*, where he'd read that Wodehouse had written over ninety books. "What would you like to drink?" he said before Millie had time to confuse him with another subject.

"Organic spicy ginger," she said.

Bob walked to the counter and returned with two identical cups of tea and a plateful of cookies. All the ladies in the room watched Bob as he collected his order. Many of the residents of the Easy Rest Retirement Village weighed more than the life-insurance charts said they should, but not Bob. He was tall and slender, and his face reminded the ladies of the late John Wayne. Millie saw this similarity, but she would've preferred the features of Marcello Mastroianni.

Nonetheless, Bob was attractive, and Millie thought he might not be as stupid as he appeared. "Other than Wodehouse, what else do you do with your time?" she asked.

Bob saw the danger in this question. He wondered if the Prairie Flower Bookstore might buy back *Money for Nothing*. "What do you do with yours?" he asked.

"I write poetry," Millie said. "Do you like poetry?"

"Love it." Bob hadn't read a poem since he graduated from high school.

"That's nice. What poets do you like?"

Holy crap, Bob thought. What next? He tried to remember the poetry he'd read in school. "Robert First," he said.

"Robert First?"

"Yes. Remember the one about the doctor in a blizzard?"

Millie looked at Bob as she tried to remember poems about doctors and blizzards. "I'm not familiar with that," she said.

"I'll google it," Bob said. "After I find it, we can get together again."

If this prospect thrilled Millie, she didn't look thrilled. "All right," she said.

Once he'd returned to his apartment, Bob sat down at his Dell laptop, typed "robert first" in the search box, and hit "enter." This summoned, among other things, the First State Bank of St. Robert, Missouri, and an orthopedic surgeon in Concord, Massachusetts, but Google revealed nothing about a doctor in a blizzard.

Bob finally realized that literature wouldn't lead him to success with Millie. He'd have to do too much homework. He needed a new subject, something he already understood. He turned off the computer and walked to the Easy Rest Library, where he grabbed a recent copy of *The Wall Street Journal*. He looked through the pages until he came to an article he knew something about.

The story dealt with U.S. monetary policy. The Department of the Treasury was, the *Journal* said, printing money as fast as possible. Bob saw the danger in this. It could lead to inflation, raising the price of organic spicy ginger to fifty dollars per cup.

Once again, Bob met Millie at the Wee Cup Tea Shoppe. "I have an idea," he said, after first obtaining the tea and cookies.

Millie looked at him dubiously. "Go ahead. Tell me about it."

"Do you know what the Bureau of Engraving and Printing does?"

"Let me guess," Millie said. "It prints money. Then the Federal Reserve Banks funnel that money into the economy."

Bob saw that he now had Millie's attention. "What happens if they print too much money?"

"That's debatable. It might stimulate the economy. It might cause inflation. Or it might do both. What's your idea, Bob?"

"Ah," Bob said. "I'm glad you asked. I know how to limit the printing of new money. You simply pass a law that regulates the amount of ink delivered to the Bureau of Engraving and Printing. No ink, no money."

Bob sat back in his chair and waited. Millie looked at him as you might look at your brother-in-law when he asks you to lend him ten thousand dollars.

Millie looked at her watch. "I have to go," she said. She stood up and rushed out the door. Bob sat there, staring out the window. In the distance, workers were erecting identical houses, all of which were identically ugly. Bob thought they were beautiful, far more attractive than the cornfields they replaced.

He picked up one of the cookies, took a bite, and chewed thoughtfully. He rarely had ideas, and Millie had seemed uninterested. Her loss and my gain, he told himself.

Bob returned the book to the Prairie Flower Bookstore and used the proceeds to pay part of his next cable-television bill. Then he went back to his normal routine. He played golf, watched television, and read the sports section of the *Chicago Tribune*. He found no reason to spend any more time at the Wee Cup Tea Shoppe.

After breakfast each morning, Bob went to the library and caught up on the news. How were the Cubs, Sox, Bears, and Bulls doing? Who was under investigation for use of performance-enhancing drugs? Who, if anyone, had accepted bribes to alter the outcome of a game or tournament?

One day, as he went to the office to pay his rent, Bob saw a potential resident talking to Alicia Fogerty, the manager. He sat down in the foyer and pretended to read a news magazine that lay with others on a white table made of imitation wood. The new woman was attractive, almost as attractive as Millie, which was good enough for Bob. "Stella," the manager said to the woman, "I think you'll love it here. Let me show you the apartment."

The two women walked away, and Bob decided to await their return, which left him with the news magazine to entertain himself. He flipped through the pages until he came to a story about a group of Icelandic students. The attorney general of Wisconsin had become suspicious of these students, who met every Thursday evening at a bar near the University of Wisconsin in Madison.

The attorney general had created a list of reasons for investigating the students. First of all, while at the bar, they spoke only in Icelandic. The students claimed that they were simply trying to help preserve their native language, but neither Bob nor the attorney general believed them. They both believed that the students had formed an Icelandic sleeper cell.

As part of this investigation, the attorney general had obtained a warrant and his agents had searched the apartments in which the students lived. They had recovered Icelandic textbooks, Icelandic dictionaries, and Icelandic flags. They also found photographs of the students, all of whom had blond hair, blue eyes, and straight teeth.

At this point, according to the article, the press took off with the story. A columnist for the *Milwaukee Journal Sentinel* called the students the "Icelandic sleepy cell," armed with unlimited snowballs and a language that almost no one else would ever learn. He pointed out that Iceland had no standing army, and it had a population less than the city of Omaha.

After the new resident came back to the office and signed the lease, Bob intercepted her as she headed toward the exit. "You're new here, aren't you?" he said. The woman responded with a smile and revealed her name, which was Stella Bird. Her dark-brown hair reminded Bob of Jane Russell in *The Outlaw*, although Russell had revealed more of her upper body than one expected to see at the Easy Rest Retirement Village. By the time Stella said goodbye, Bob had arranged a date at the Wee Cup Tea Shoppe. He hoped she'd never heard of P.G. Wodehouse.

One week later, after Stella had moved into her new apartment, Bob carried two cups of coffee over to a table by the window. "Stella," he said, "have you heard about the terrorists in Madison?"

"Madison? No," she said. "Tell me about them."

In less than five minutes, Bob recapitulated everything he could remember about the sleeper cell. Stella had not walked away or changed the subject. She either believed or pretended to believe everything Bob said, and she continued to stare at his handsome face as though he weren't an imbecile. "Bob," she said, "what a frightening story. What will these people do next?"

"I don't know, but I plan to stay informed."

"How?"

Bob hesitated. "I'll google them every day."

"Brilliant," Stella said. "Keep me up to date."

"I will. We should meet every afternoon to discuss the latest news."

"How about every night? We could then make any moves needed."

Bob thought of some moves he'd like to make. "Absolutely," he said. "See you tomorrow."

"How about tonight?" At her age, which was fifty-seven, Stella didn't like to wait for anything. Life was passing, and she wanted to grab every opportunity that fell into her lap.

"Absolutely," Bob said. At eight o'clock that evening, Bob met Stella at her apartment, where they talked about the Icelandic sleepy cell for thirty seconds. Then they slipped into bed. Bob had taken a miracle pill at six o'clock, and Stella had applied various creams and ointments. They were well oiled and ready to go.

"Stella," Bob said as his hand explored her smooth thighs. "I tried to get friendly with another woman here, but I dropped her in favor of you. She never had any ideas. All she ever talked about was books."

"Some people are like that," Stella said. She put her hand on Bob's cheek and kissed him. "It's a waste of time trying to help them. They're not like us. They don't have a clue."

MAYAN
FINALE

If you've glanced at the Mayan calendar hanging on your kitchen wall lately, you probably noticed that the world didn't end on December 21, 2012. I didn't know anything about it myself, but Sally Barber told me the entire universe would end on that date, and we might as well break out the champagne right then because it would all be over before we got the chance to sing "Auld Lang Syne" when the next year rolled around. And if you wanted to kiss someone under the mistletoe, you'd have to pucker up before the earth's crust fell apart.

I asked Sally if she'd like a kiss right then, but she said not if the world depended on it and she'd rather kiss a toad if she had to make a choice. So I said she could have it however she wanted it and not to come to me for sympathy when the South Pole suddenly poked out of the snow in Wisconsin.

Sally said, "Good luck, loser," and walked away before I could ask her if we could hold hands instead of kissing a toad. Anyway, I could see I'd have to find out about the end of the world if I was going to hang out with Sally. I found a magazine article at the library, but it was too long, and reading usually makes me go to sleep anyway. So I sat down at one of the library's computers and began looking through YouTube with combinations of words and numbers like "Mayan," "December 21," and "sayonara."

It took a while, but I finally found something that told me what I needed. Some of the people who'd got themselves all in a dither about this galactic blowout thought that the upcoming Mayan disaster would give all of us a swell opportunity to transform our consciousness, and we could all look forward to having indigenous insights, although YouTube didn't say what that means. While we were at it, we could stop worrying about the planet Nibiru smashing into the Earth and turning all of us into space dust. If you've never heard of Nibiru, it just goes to show that you haven't been paying attention to the Mayan calendar right there beside the Frigidaire.

According to the Nibiru deniers, the world wouldn't end on December 21. Instead, a new age would begin. We'd have the opportunity to get back to the land and find new careers as bee keepers, fish farmers, and manure haulers. Just think how much better that would be than all the crap you swim through every day at the job you have now.

After watching all this on YouTube, I got tired and couldn't force myself to look up the people who thought the world would simply fall apart December 21. Then one of the guys who live at the bus depot told me I could sneak into the movie theater down the street and watch this show about how the world was going to end. He said it had lots of explosions, laser battles, and all the other stuff you see in the movies these days.

The movie was called *Mayan Finale*, and what I really wanted was some facts about the world and when it would end and what to do about it. I thought that if I could find out how to keep Sally Barber and me alive, she might like me a little more. She might even knock it off with the toad jokes.

But the movie had nothing in it like what I wanted. It showed how the trouble was going to begin when this space object banged into New Jersey, which would then throw the Earth off its axis and get it spinning and wobbling until it all started falling apart, with New Jersey and California and everything else flying off like a pile of pancakes on a roller coaster.

So that's how it was supposed to end, but someone must have miscalculated the date. So all we have to do is recalculate it, and we'll go through the whole thing again. That's how all the holy-roller preachers do it when they predict the end of the world. They say they got the date wrong, but watch out next time. We won't know for sure until we wake up on the day of the big event. If we don't wake up, it'll be too late to start keeping bees.

PATRICK IRELAN is the author of *Reruns*, his first collection of short stories. His other publications include two family memoirs: *Central Standard* and *A Firefly in the Night*. Irelan is the father of two daughters. He lives in Iowa.

The Ice Cube Press began publishing in 1993 to focus on how to live with the natural world and to better understand how people can best live together in the communities they share and inhabit. Using the literary arts to explore life and experiences in the heartland of the United States we have been recognized by a number of well-known writers including: Gary Snyder, Gene Logsdon, Wes Jackson, William Pitt Root, Patricia Hampl, Greg Brown, Jim Harrison, Annie Dillard, Ken Burns, Kathleen Norris, Janisse Ray, Craig Lesley, Alison Deming, Richard Rhodes, Michael Pollan, and Barry Lopez. We've published a number of well-known authors including: Mary Swander, Jim Heynen, Mary Pipher, Paul Engle, William Stafford, James Hearst, Bill Holm, Connie Mutel, John T. Price, Carol Bly, Marvin Bell, Debra Marquart, Ted Kooser, Stephanie Mills, Bill McKibben, and Paul Gruchow. We have won several publishing awards over the last twenty years. Check out our books at our web site, join our facebook group, follow us on twitter, visit booksellers, museum shops, or any place you can find good books and discover why we continue striving to, "hear the other side."

Ice Cube Press, LLC (est. 1993)
205 N. Front Street
North Liberty, Iowa 52317-9302
steve@icecubepress.com
twitter @icecubepress
www.icecubepress.com

I know two miracles,
& they are obvious to the eye & soul
Laura Lee & Fenna Marie